5.99

DMU 0364440 01 6

D1101532

Withdrawn

Lincolnshire College of Agriculture a
Library
Caythorpe

THE
BYERLEY
TURK

To Damien, Kate and Jane

THE BYERLEY TURK

*Three centuries of the
tail male racing lines*

K. M. Haralambos

 THRESHOLD BOOKS

First published in 1990
by Threshold Books
The Kenilworth Press Limited
661 Fulham Road, London SW6 5PZ

Copyright © K.M. Haralambos 1990

Designed by Alan Hamp
Picture research by Sarah Waters

All rights reserved.
No part of this publication may be reproduced,
stored in a retrieval system, or transmitted, in any
form or by any means, electronic, mechanical,
photo-copying, recording, or otherwise, without
written permission of the publisher.

British Library Cataloguing in Publication Data
Haralambos, K. M.
    The Byerley Turk: three centuries of the tail male
    racing lines.
    1. Racehorses
    I. Title
    636.1'2

ISBN 0—901366—19—6

Typeset by Falcon Graphic Art Ltd,
Wallington, Surrey.
Printed and bound in Great Britain by
Westway Offset, Wembley.

Contents

6 *Contents*

Illustrations

Illustration acknowledgements
The publishers are grateful to the following for permission to reproduce the illustrations on
the pages noted: By Gracious Permission of Her Majesty The Queen 35 (bottom), 38;
Arthur Ackermann & Son Ltd 89; P. Bertrand et Fils 124, 129, 131; *Blood Horse* Magazine
45, 48, 49, 57; The Trustees of the British Museum 22; Gerry Cranham Front cover (top);
The Earl of Derby/photo E.T. Archive 71; E.T. Archive Front cover (centre), 18 (top), 36
(top), 94, 108; Mary Evans Picture Library, 116; the Halifax Collection 72; Dell Hancock
Photography 58, 60; *The Illustrated London News* Picture Library 80; the Stewards of the
Jockey Club 28-9, 97, 101, 108, 110; The Mansell Collection 20, 24, 32, 70; Laurie Morton
152, 153; The National Horseracing Museum, Newmarket 76, 151; The National Museum
of Racing and Hall of Fame, Saratoga Springs 102 (top); The National Stud 152;
Newmarket Library, Racing Collection 81, 84, 95; W.W. Rouch & Co 99, 103, 122, 126
142, 143, 149; The Reverend Christopher Seale 35 (top), Société d'Encouragement pour
l'Amélioration des Races de Chevaux 102 (bottom); S & G Press Agency 127, 135, 136, 146,
150, 159, 161, 164; Sportpix, Australia Front cover (bottom), 158; Tate Gallery, London
44; Tattersalls 36 (bottom), 68; Fiona Vigors 151 (bottom); Derek Wrightson Photo 17, 18
(bottom), 26, 27, 28; York Racing Museum and Library 34, 39, 40, 66, 67 (bottom); The
Marquess of Zetland 102 (bottom).

Acknowledgements

One morning when the spring sun was shining on the Park, once part of Goldsborough Manor, I looked out of the window and wondered if the Byerley family, whose domain it was in the seventeenth century, had any connection with a stallion of which I had read. In my mind's eye I could see him galloping just beyond the fence, and there and then I determined to trace his descendants, if any.

Of horses I knew little, of thoroughbreds – nothing. It is due to the kindness, patience and enthusiasm of so many people, including owners, breeders, trainers and jockeys that I have been able to conclude the search. Inevitably, because of space restrictions, I have had to omit some stallions who are equally as important as those mentioned. For this I apologise.

To all who have helped in a variety of ways I extend my sincere thanks, especially to Frank Berry, Ray Townsend and C.J. Dennis without whose generous help and encouragement I should have fallen by the wayside. Acknowledgements are due to Peter Willett for giving his time and expertise to assess the typescript and to David Wright for checking it, together with his initial help which set me on the right road. Also to Michael Formby; Mr and Mrs R.E. Bromet; the Oliver family; Gillian Wood; Dede Marks, of the York Horse Racing Museum; The National Horse Racing Museum, Newmarket; The National Stud, Newmarket; The Irish National Stud; The Right Honourable The Earl of Derby; The Embassy of the United Arab Emirates, London; Haras du Pin (Service des Haras Nationaux); Gestüt Harzburg, Hanover, and Klaus Kolitsch; The Keeneland Library, Lexington; The Thoroughbred Record Breeders' Pedigree Service, Lexington; Elmer E. Horsey, Shoshone Farm, Florida; Herr Peter Schmanns, Isernhagen, W. Germany.

My appreciation also goes to Lois Pertee for photocopying, to Belinda Yarrow for so cheerfully producing the typescript, and to Denise Gibson for her work in preparing the final manuscript for submission to the publishers.

In conclusion, it is not only enjoyment that has been derived from tracing the dynasty. Along the way I have come to acknowledge that

'Animals of the horse kind deserve a place next to man in a history of nature . . . their activity, their strength, their usefulness and their beauty render them the principal objects of our curiosity and care.' (Goldsmith's *Animated Nature*.)

K.M. Haralambos
The Lodge
Goldsborough
January 1989

Author's Note
Where the name of a horse is printed in italics, this is not an indication that that horse belongs to a particular category or grade. It is intended to show it as being of some particular importance – perhaps for achievements on the racecourse, as a sire, for outstanding qualities of character – or for some other aspect of its story that seemed to me to merit special attention.

Dates shown on the blood-line charts refer to the year foaled unless otherwise indicated.

Bibliography

Blunt, Lady Anne. *A Pilgrimage to Nejd*. John Murray, 1881.

Dixon, Henry Hall. The 'Druid' Sporting Library: *The Post and the Paddock* and *Silk and Scarlet*. Vuiton & Co. 1895.

Fleming, Mary. *Lexington and his Dynasty* (from The Thoroughbred of California, October 1975).

Greely, Margaret. *Arabian Exodus*. J.A. Allen, 1975.

Harewood, Lord. *The Lonsdale Library, Flat Racing*. Seeley Service & Co. Ltd., 1940

Hewitt, Abram S. *Sire Lines*. Thoroughbred Owners' and Breeders' Association, USA.

Jones, Michael Wynne. *The Derby*. Croom Helm.

Leicester, Sir Charles. *Bloodstock Breeding*. J.A. Allen, 1964 (new edition).

Meysey Thompson, Col. R.F. *Reminiscences of The Court, The Camp and The Chase*. Edward Arnold, 1898.

Mortimer, Roger with Tim Neligan. *The Epsom Derby*. Michael Joseph, 1984.

Mortimer, Roger, Onslow, Richard and Willett, Peter. *Biographical Encyclopaedia of British Flat Racing*. Macdonald and Janes, 1978.

Pick, William, *Matches, etc. run for at York 1709*.

Pick, William. *Turf Register and Stud Book, Volume I* (1803).

Reynolds, James. *A World of Horses* (Hutchinson).

Ross, Michael (Editor). *Directory of the Turf*. The Sporting Life.

Seth-Smith, Michael and Mortimer, Roger. *Derby 200*. Guinness Superlatives Ltd, 1979.

Seth-Smith, Michael (Editor). *History of Flat Racing*. New English Library, 1978.

Racing Calendars from 1790. James Weatherby.

Sires. Pacemaker Publications (various dates).

The Blood Horse Stallion Register, USA (to 1987).

The Stallion Book. Weatherby's.

Tail Male Racing Lines of the Byerley Turk

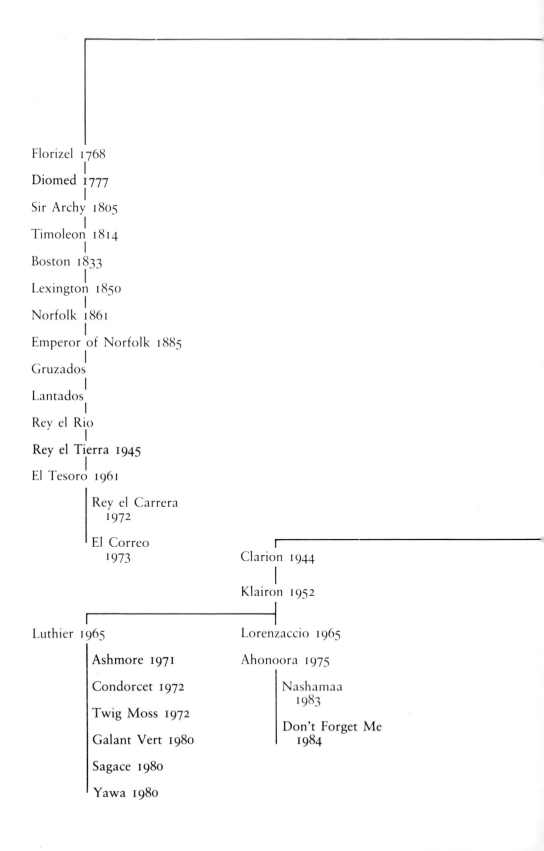

Florizel 1768

Diomed 1777

Sir Archy 1805

Timoleon 1814

Boston 1833

Lexington 1850

Norfolk 1861

Emperor of Norfolk 1885

Gruzados

Lantados

Rey el Rio

Rey el Tierra 1945

El Tesoro 1961

Rey el Carrera
1972

El Correo
1973

Clarion 1944

Klairon 1952

Luthier 1965

Lorenzaccio 1965

Ashmore 1971

Condorcet 1972

Twig Moss 1972

Galant Vert 1980

Sagace 1980

Yawa 1980

Ahonoora 1975

Nashamaa
1983

Don't Forget Me
1984

The Byerley Turk c. 1680 – Jigg c. 1701 – Partner 1718 – Tartar 1743

Herod 1758

Woodpecker 1773

Buzzard 1787

Selim 1802

Sultan 1816

Bay Middleton 1833

The Flying Dutchman 1846

Dollar 1860

Androcles 1870

Cambyse 1884

Gardefeu 1895

Chouberski 1902

Brûleur 1910

Ksar 1918

Tourbillon 1928

Djebel 1937

continued overleaf

Hugh Lupus 1952

Hethersett 1959

Blakeney 1966

Julio Mariner 1975

Sexton Blake 1975

Tyrnavos 1977

Dihistan 1982

Commodore
Blake 1977

Baron Blakeney 1977

Electric 1979

Rarity 1967

Decent Fellow 1973

Pollerton 1974

Djeddah 1945

Midsummer
Night II 1957

Jimmy Reppin
1965

Sula Bula 1978

My Babu 1945

Crozier 1958

Inverness Drive
1966

Beat Inflation
1973

Tail Male Racing Lines of the Byerley Turk

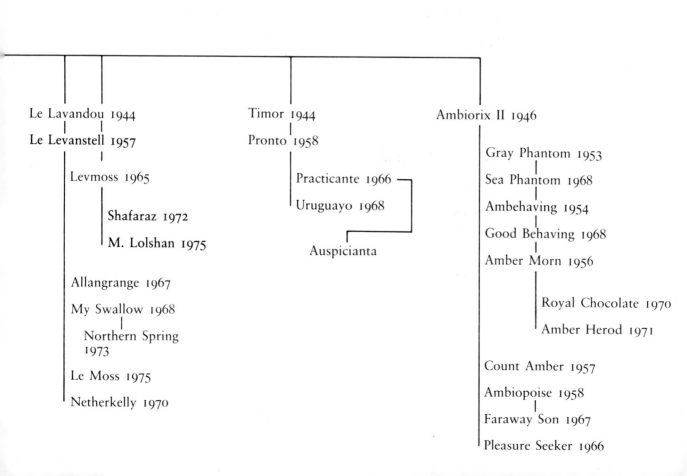

Le Lavandou 1944
Le Levanstell 1957

Levmoss 1965

Shafaraz 1972

M. Lolshan 1975

Allangrange 1967

My Swallow 1968
Northern Spring
1973

Le Moss 1975

Netherkelly 1970

Timor 1944
Pronto 1958

Practicante 1966
Uruguayo 1968

Auspicianta

Ambiorix II 1946

Gray Phantom 1953

Sea Phantom 1968

Ambehaving 1954

Good Behaving 1968

Amber Morn 1956

Royal Chocolate 1970

Amber Herod 1971

Count Amber 1957

Ambiopoise 1958

Faraway Son 1967

Pleasure Seeker 1966

Castrel 1801

Pantaloon 1824

Windhound 1847

Thormanby 1857

Atlantic 1871

Le Sancy 1884

Le Samaritain 1895

Roi Hérode 1904

The Tetrarch 1911

Tetratema 1917

Bactériophage 1929

Téléférique 1934

Torcello 1940

Nord Sud 1958

Soudard 1968

Alizier 1947

Crivelli 1961

Tapalqué 1965

Highflyer 1774

Sir Peter Teazle 1784

Sir Paul 1803

Paulowitz 1813

Cain 1822

Ion 1835

Wild Dayrell 1852

Buccaneer 1857

Kisber 1873

Flibustier 1867

Hannibal 1891

Fels 1903

Laland 1913

'Hast thou given the horse strength? Hast thou clothed his neck with thunder? Canst thou make him afraid as a grasshopper? The glory of his nostrils is terrible. He paweth in the valley and rejoiceth in his strength. He goeth on to meet the armed men. He mocketh at fear and is not affrighted; neither turneth he back from the sword. The quiver rattleth against him, the glittering spear and the shield. He swalloweth the ground with fierceness and rage . . . He saith among the trumpets "Ha, ha" and he smelleth the battle afar off, the thunder of the captains and the shouting.'

(*Job*, Chapter 39)

RIGHT Memorial window to Captain Byerley in the church at Goldsborough.

BELOW Goldsborough Hall, the home of Captain Robert Byerley.

The Byerley Turk, by John Wootton.

The paddock at Goldsborough Hall where the Byerley Turk was kept.

PART ONE

'Foyal et Loyal'

1 | War-Horse

WHERE HE FIRST drew breath, this 'star of the desert, drinker of the wind'*, we shall never know. Arab, Turk or Barb is still a matter of conjecture – but, history and legend mingled, this is the story of the Byerley Turk.

There docked one day in 1688 in the city of Portsmouth a ship bearing Captain Robert Byerley and his independently-raised troop of cavalry. Attached to the army of the Duke of Lorraine, they had been fighting in Hungary to defend Christendom from the incursion of Turkish infidels. They had won a notable victory at Buda and brought with them considerable spoils of war. That portion accorded to the Captain was a fiery Arab stallion, the like of which had seldom, if ever, been seen in England. The horse, with his elegance, handsome build, speed and fire, was the envy of the officers of the Queen Dowager's Cuirassiers, which regiment the Captain joined, whose stockier mounts compared very unfavourably with the excellence of the Turk.

The regiment, now incorporated into the 6th Dragoon Guards, was sent in 1689 to join the forces of King William of Orange in Ireland, Robert taking with him his dark bay charger. The Byerley motto 'Foyal et Loyal' (faithful and loyal) applied appropriately enough to both horse and rider. Captain Byerley fought with courage and panache. Reconnoitring before the Battle of the Boyne, he was surprised by a troop of King James II's cavalry and was in danger of encirclement. But the Turk was a war-horse and swiftly carried his new master to safety.

Undoubtedly, his superior speed saved Byerley's life for he could almost 'fly without wings'. Robert was promoted to Colonel of the Regiment and at the cessation of hostilities he returned home with his stallion to Middridge Grange, Durham, and Goldsborough Hall, near Knaresborough, where he was Lord of the Manor. In 1693 he married Mary Wharton, the sole heir of Philip Wharton. This unfortunate lady had endured an enforced marriage to the younger brother of Archibald, first Duke of Argyll. It was dissolved by an Act of Parliament circa 1690. By all accounts the second marriage was a happy one. They had five children, Robert, Philip, Anne, Mary and Elizabeth.

* Attributed to the Prophet Mohammed.

OPPOSITE
'Horse match between Charles II and Henry Jermyn at Newmarket in 1684.' Engraving after Francis Barrow.

Die Haubt stadt Ofen
Wie solche von der Christl: Armee Bela...

A die Juden u. Wasser stadt.
B die Obere Vorstad C unter Vorstadt.
D kleine Vorstadt. E Schloß kirche.
F Gefängnus der Gefang Christen.
G Bassa kirche H Bassa Joannis Rundel.
K Neu erbaute Türckische kirche.
L Erd=Thor M Sieg kirch.
N die Kirche worauf die Stad Uhr.
O eine Alte kirche.
P Mustapha Bassa Rundel.
Q Warme Bäder.
R Keyser u Reichs Auxiliar
        Völcker Attacque.
S Chur Beyersche.
.... Sächs: Attacque.
..... Brandenb:)
T Anlauff u. Sturm.
V Gesprengte Minen.
X Brechen.

Anno 1686.

Inter Ungarn,
und Glücklich Erobert.

PEST.

Gerhards
Berg

DONAU Fl. Schloß

PREVIOUS PAGE
The Battle of Buda
from a contemporary
print (1686).

No doubt Robert and his 'Byerley's Treasure' as he became known, were happy to be in the peaceful rural retreat of Goldsborough, surrounded by elms and the lush pastures of the Manor. In Ireland offers of up to three thousand guineas, a vast sum, had been made for the stallion, and refused. Little did the Captain imagine the fame his horse was to achieve; for with the Darley Arabian and the Godolphin Arabian he was to become the progenitor of all British Thoroughbred stock. Although he had never raced, the Byerley Turk proved an excellent sire of quality racehorses. Unfortunately, according to Pick's *Turf Register*, 'He did not cover many well-bred mares'. Mating in those days was not the refined science of modern times.

Robert Byerley became Member of Parliament for Durham and for Knaresborough in nine parliaments between 1697 and 1710. He died

in 1714 at the age of fifty-four, and was buried in the Chancel of Goldsborough Church where a handsome memorial was erected to the whole family. None of his children had issue and so this branch of the Byerley family is heard of no more. But the dynasty of the Byerley Turk endures to the present day.

Generally on the raw-boned side, horses of the Byerley Turk line were not, in the early days, noted for their beauty, though their fiery disposition and strength carried them to many a victory. Of the Turk's offspring, Sprite, Black Hearty and Basto were his best runners, but it was *Jigg* who carried on the line. A common stallion standing in Lincolnshire, he was out of a daughter of Spanker (by the D'Arcy Yellow Turk out of an untraceable mare). Then in 1718 *Partner*, a chesnut colt with a star and stripe and two white hind stockings, was foaled. He was bred by Sir

The Battle of the Boyne, fought in July 1690.

The Byerley memorial
in Goldsborough
Church.

Captain Byerley and his wife. Detail from the Byerley memorial.

Captain Byerley's tombstone in Goldsborough Church.

Charles Pelham in Lincolnshire. His dam was an own sister to the Mixbury Galloway. He was a game little 13.2hh pony, who won races at York and various other courses in the North of England.

Partner was a colt with a fine turn of speed. He was raced at Newmarket where he triumphed in all but one of his outings. He became the best racehorse of his day and, with his unrivalled power, looks and virility, he was judged to be the finest stallion in the land. He went to stud in 1728 but by 1732 he was being reserved for mares owned by a group of friends, the most influential of whom was a Mr Croft.

The most famous of Partner's offspring was undoubtedly *Tartar*, also originally named Partner, who was out of Miliora by Fox. This good-looking bay colt was bred by Mr Leedes of North Milford, in Yorkshire, and foaled in 1743. When fully grown he stood just short of 15hh. As a five-year-old he won races at Beverley, Malton and York. He was then sold to the Duke of Ancaster, who was delighted at his victory in the King's Plate at Lichfield and his wins at Guildford and Newmarket in the following year. He had a good record as a stallion, siring horses of quality, his most famous offspring being *Herod*. Tartar stood at Oulston, Easingwold, at Anthony Smith's stables, the fee being two guineas a mare and two shillings the man. This rose to five guineas, and five shillings to the groom, before his death in 1759. He was advertised as, 'The famous strong Chestnut Horse Tartar . . . . 15 hands high and free from blemish.'

'View of the Noblemens and Gentlemens several Strings or Trains of Running Horses, taking their Exercise up by ye Watering Course on the Warren Hill, at New Market. . .' Print after Peter Tillemans.

2 | Old Rowley

KING CHARLES II (1630–1685) was keenly interested in the racing and breeding of Thoroughbred horses. He was the only English king to have ridden a winner at Newmarket. During his exile in France and Belgium, he acquired considerable knowledge of the Arab and Barbary breeds which were being offered for sale, particularly at Toulon.

On his return he commissioned his Master of the Horse to purchase from abroad mares for the Royal Stables which were established at Newmarket. It was due to his great interest and patronage that town and heath became an important centre for the sport.

The elder of two sons borne by Nell Gwynn to the King was accorded the title of the Duke of St Albans (1670–1726). It is about his association with the Byerley Turk that the following tale is told. It happened at Newmarket on the occasion of the first running of 'Old Rowley's Cup'. Old Rowley was the King's hack and his subjects affectionately dubbed their sovereign Old Rowley, too.

The sporting Duke of St Albans attended the meeting in his usual extravagant manner, arriving in a grandly caparisoned coach with his arms emblazoned on the door panels. It was drawn by four mettlesome Barbs, heavier than racehorses but highly suitable for their task.

The Duke sauntered among the racegoers gathered round the betting stall, greeting one here, one there. They expressed their surprise that he had not entered a horse. He explained that he had returned to England only the day before and had been unaware that the race was to be run. 'But,' he said, 'I have a horse to win this race. Get me a good rider.' The off-lead horse from his coach was unhitched and a rider was found. The Duke removed a sash from around his waist, tied it diagonally across the jockey's shirt and away they went.

That is how Old Rowley's Cup was won by Old Rowley's son with a coach-horse named Scatter, by Plunder, whose sire was the Byerley Turk.

PART TWO

The Herod Dynasty

The Duke of Cumberland

TWO NOBLEMEN, the Duke of Ancaster and the Duke of Cumberland, were the instigators of Herod's conception. Tartar, his sire, was owned by the Duke of Ancaster, and his dam Cypron, by Blaze, belonged to the Duke of Cumberland. The latter, christened William Augustus, and accorded the title of Duke of Cumberland (1721–65), was the second surviving son of King George II. He was a resolute if unfortunate soldier, who was severely wounded at the age of twenty-two while serving with the army at the battle of Dettingen. His wounds healed, he was appointed Captain General of the allied army in Flanders in 1745, and on his return to England was put in charge of the campaign to defeat Prince Charles, the young Pretender. He earned his nickname 'Butcher Cumberland' for the ferocity with which he crushed the rebellion. The slaughter at Culloden over, the Duke set sail for Europe once more, where he commanded the Hanoverian army. But after two crushing defeats at Hastenbeck and Klosterzeven, he returned to England, his military career at an end.

The Duke then took up the post of Ranger of Windsor Forest, living at Cumberland Lodge where he established his stud. He was the most influential horse breeder of his time, for he was instrumental in establishing the development of the British Thoroughbred. Through his two home-bred stallions, Eclipse, a descendant of the Darley Arabian, and Herod, the excellence of the two dynasties was assured.

The Duke was a great sportsman and a compulsive gambler. He frequently played cards until dawn and rarely ventured out without dice in his pocket so that he could enjoy a 'throw or two' during a lull in the proceedings. He was easy meat for the sharks at Newmarket but, despite considerable losses he persisted in his aim of creating the finest stud in England. Money was no object. He also secured for Ascot a reputation for racing which has endured to the present time.

Herod, at first called King Herod, was a bay colt foaled in 1758. According to Pick's *Turf Register* he was 'one of the best bred horses this kingdom ever produced'. One can imagine him proudly pacing the rides of Windsor Forest. His first race at Newmarket was in October

OPPOSITE
The Duke of Cumberland (1721-65), by David Morier.

The entry for King Herod in *William Pick's Racing Calendar* (1709–85).

KING HEROD,

(A BAY HORSE—FOALED IN 1758,)

Bred by His Royal Highnefs WILLIAM Duke of CUMBERLAND, ana sola to Sir JOHN MOORE, Bart.

KING HEROD was got by Tartar, *(page 99)*; out of *Cypron.*

At Newmarket in October, 1763, KING HEROD beat the Duke of Ancafter's Roman, by Blank, 8ft. 7lb. B. C. 500gs. At Newmarket in April, 1764, He won a Sweepftakes of 300gs each, h. ft. (9 fubfcribers) 10ft. B. C. beating Sir John Moore's (afterwards Mr. Wildman's) Tartar, by Tartar, out of Mifs Meredith :—At ftarting, 2 to 1 on King Herod. At Afcot-Heath in June, KING HEROD 8ft. 13lb. beat Lord Rockingham's Tom Tinker, by Sampfon, 8ft. 7lb. four miles, 1000gs.—4 to 1 on King Herod. At Newmarket in October, KING HEROD, 8ft. 11lb. beat the Duke of Grafton's An. tinous, 8ft. 8lb. B. C 500gs.—6 to 4 on Antinous. At Newmarket in May, 1765, KING HEROD, 9ft. beat the Duke of Grafton's Antinous, 8ft. 5lb. B. C. 1000gs.—7 to 5 on Antinous. In October, at 9ft. He was beat by Sir James Lowther's Afcham, 6 years old, 8ft. B. C. 1000gs.—3 to 1 on King Herod. At the deceafe of his Royal Highnefs, KING HEROD was purchafed by Sir John Moore; and in April, 1766, at 9ft. He was beat by Lord Bolingbroke's Turf, 5 yrs old, 8ft. 8lb. B. C. 1000gs.—At ftarting, 7 to 4 on King Herod. At York in Auguft, He ftarted for the Subfcription-Purfe againft Bay Malton, Jerkin, Royal George, Flylax, and Beaufremont; but a blood-veffel burft in King Herod's head, when running the laft mile, which caufed him to be taken dangeroufly ill, and prevented his coming in a better place than laft. At Newmarket in April,1767, KING HEROD was fecond to Bay Malton, beating Turf and Afcham. *See Bay Malton's Performances.* And in May, at 5ft. 7lb. He beat Mr. Shaflo's Afcham, 6ft. B. C. 1000gs.—6 to 4 on Afcham. The above were the only times of King Herod's running.

1763 over a course of a little more than four miles. He beat the Duke of Ancaster's Roman for 500 guineas. The following year saw him twice beating the Duke of Grafton's Antinous, no mean rival and the favourite to win, on the Beacon course.

The Duke of Cumberland's indulgence led to excessive corpulence, which with his old war wounds contributed to his early death at the age of forty-four. Herod was sold to Sir John Moore and continued

Old Partner, from a 1755 print.

The Duke of Cumberland visiting his stud at Windsor. The painting by Sawrey Gilpin and William Marlow, shows the Duke with his mares and foals near the Long Walk.

King Herod, by John Wootton (1758).

Highflyer by John Boultbee, with Highflyer Hall in the background. Richard Tattersall named the Hall in honour of his horse.

KING HEROD was a remarkable fine horfe, with uncommon power, and allowed to be one of the beft bred Horfes this kingdom ever produced, and as a Stallion inferior to none, being fire of a larger number of Racers, Stallions, and Brood-Mares than any other Horfe either before or fince his time.

THE SONS AND DAUGHTERS
OF KING HEROD WON AS FOLLOW, VIZ.

			£	s.
In 1771	1 winner won		525	0
1772	4 winners won		3,890	10
1773	17 winners won		6,680	10
1774	23 winners won		10,206	6
1775	17 winners won		7,744	0
1776	19 winners won		9,172	6
1777	35 winners won		15,773	14
1778	45 winners won		23,046	5
1779	50 winners won		21,396	2
1780	55 winners won		20,008	15
1781	53 winners won		21,087	10
1782	50 winners won		18,605	18
1783	47 winners won		15,629	1
1784	34 winners won		15,998	2
1785	27 winners won		9,224	5
1786	11 winners won		1,777	5
1787	6 winners won		514	0
1788	1 winner won		105	0
1789	2 winners won		121	0

In 19 years   497 winners won   £ 201,505   9

BESIDES THE ABOVE SUMS,

In 1774, At Newmarket, 6 Hogfheads of Claret, by Telemachus;
In 1778, At Newmarket, 14 Hogfheads of Claret, by Bourdeux; and
2 by Laburnum, (the fecond horfe);
In 1779, At Newmarket, 6 Hogfheads of Claret, by Sting;
In 1780, At Newmarket, 9 Hogfheads of Claret, by Buccaneer;
In 1781, At Newmarket, the Clermont Cup, by Woodpecker;
In 1782, At Salifbury, the City Silver Bowl, by Epfom;
In 1783, At Newmarket, the Whip, by Anvil;
In 1784, At Newmarket, 5 Hogfheads of Claret, by Gonzales; and
2 by Balance, (the fecond horfe); and
In 1786, At Salifbury, the City Silver Bowl, by Challenger.

There might be more winners of KING HEROD's get, than the above, but they are unknown to the Publifher.

The achievements of the sons and daughters of King Herod listed in *William Pick's Racing Calendar.*

Cypron with her brood by Sawrey Gilpin, 1764. Her son, King Herod, with his groom, is in the background.

to run well for him until August 1765. Then he ran in the Subscription Purse at York. He was going well, when suddenly his nose began to bleed profusely – he had burst a blood vessel. He finished the race, but was last of five runners, and he was desperately ill for a time. It was thought that he would not recover but, thanks to the skill and patience of his handlers, he was able to run in two races the following spring.

Thereafter he stood at stud at Neather Hall, near Bury St Edmunds, for a fee of 10 guineas. This was later raised to 25 guineas, a fee he commanded for the rest of his life. He sired the winners of 1,042 races worth £201,505, but his greatest achievement was in fathering *Highflyer*. He and

two other sons, *Florizel* and *Woodpecker*, assured the continuance of the Byerley Turk line. Two more sons, *Fortitude* and *Justice*, are noted only for siring Derby winners. The former sired John Bull, the winner in 1792, while the latter's two sons, Rhadamanthus and Daedalus, were successful in 1790 and 1794.

Herod was the leading sire of winners eight times and it is regrettable that he lived too soon for many of his progeny to feature in the Classic races, although his daughters Bridget, Faith, and Maid of the Oaks, won three of the first five runnings of the Oaks, and his son Phenomenon won the St Leger in 1783. Herod was a truly great sire.

King Herod's progeny,
from *William Pick's
Racing Calendar*.

The following, besides a great many others, were got by KING
HEROD, viz.

Adamant,	Fortitude,	Postmaster,
Adrastus,	Frigate,	Posthumous,
Aladin,	Glancer,	Prince,
Alamahatamaha,	Gnatcatcher,	Prince Ferdinand,
Alexis,	Golden-Dun,	Prince Herod,
Antagonist,	Greylegs,	Prospect,
Antipas,	Guido,	Punch,
Anvil,	Guildford,	Quicksand,
Argos,	Hammer,	Ranger,
Ascot,	Herodotus,	Rammer,
Ashton,	Heron,	Rantipole,
Athenais,	Highflyer,	Rebel,
Balance,	Hudibras,	Rosalba,
Boston,	Il'mio,	Rosemary,
Bourdeaux,	Justice,	Rover,
Boxer,	King William,	Signor,
Bridget,	Langham,	Slender,
Brimstone,	Latona,	Snake,
Buccaneer,	Laburnum,	Spectre,
Calash,	Magnet,	Spider,
Cashkeeper, *Farnham's* Maid of the Oaks,		Sting,
Cecilia,	Maria,	Suffolk,
Chalkstone,	Minion,	Telemachus,
Challenger,	Mistly,	Thornville,
Chequino,	Monk,	Torrent,
Clandon,	Mortonia,	Trinadado,
Dancer,	Orange,	Trotter,
Drone,	Peggy,	True-Blue,
Epaminondas,	Perdita,	Tuberose,
Epsom,	Peru,	Vengeance,
Evergreen,	Phænomenon,	Weasel,
Faith, *LordGrosvenor's* Philodor,		Wickham,
Flash,	Plunder,	Whipcord,
Florizel,	Pomona,	Woodpecker, &c. &c.

PART THREE

The American Dynasty

The Direct Line in the USA

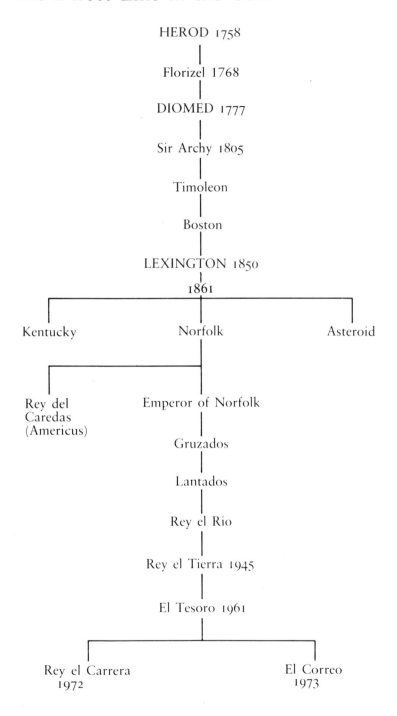

HEROD 1758

Florizel 1768

DIOMED 1777

Sir Archy 1805

Timoleon

Boston

LEXINGTON 1850

1861

Kentucky   Norfolk   Asteroid

Rey del
Caredas   Emperor of Norfolk
(Americus)

Gruzados

Lantados

Rey el Rio

Rey el Tierra 1945

El Tesoro 1961

Rey el Carrera   El Correo
1972   1973

1 | Diomed and Lexington

AMONG THE PROGENY of Herod's son Florizel were Eager, winner of the 1791 Derby, and Fidget, who produced a nameless son to win the Epsom Classic in 1797. But it is as the sire of Diomed that Florizel will be best remembered. Diomed was a lively chesnut, foaled in 1777, out of a mare by Spectator. He was sold before going into training by his breeder Richard Vernon to Sir Charles Bunbury. After winning the first running of the Derby in 1780 he was unbeaten as a three-year-old. He did well as a four-year-old but was lame the following year. He returned to racing to win the King's Plate at Guildford. However, shortly afterwards he broke down and was retired to stud.

His career as a stallion in England was not a success, and at the advanced age of twenty-one he was sold to John Hoomes for 50 guineas to be shipped to Virginia. Hardly had Diomed and John Hoomes touched dry land following their perilous voyage than the horse's astute owner sold Diomed to Colonel Miles Seddon, of Tree Hill, for 1,000 guineas. Quite convinced that he had struck a very good bargain, Hoomes was backed up by the opinion of those in the know in England who thought the stallion worthless. However, in a new land and with a new master, Diomed took on a fresh lease of life and proceeded to prove the British experts wrong.

So delighted was the Colonel with his purchase that he wrote to his friend John Taylor: 'I wish you could see Diomed – I really think him the finest horse I ever saw. He is near 16 hands and much admired by everyone who has seen him.' Though accounted of little worth in England and after making a poor start in America, due perhaps to the quality of the mares he served, Diomed proceeded to sire horses of ability for the rest of his long life. He died in 1808 at the age of thirty-one, fertile to the end.

The greatest of his sons was *Sir Archy*. Foaled in 1805, he developed into a champion racehorse. At the time of his death at the age of twenty-eight he was the leading sire of America. Among his progeny was a colt named *Timoleon*, a champion four-miler who never lost a race, but whose greatest claim to fame was in siring *Boston*. A wild individual, with a savage temperament, Boston was brilliant on the racecourse. At

Sir Charles Bunbury, owner of Diomed, with Cox his trainer, and a stable-lad. By Benjamin Marshall, c. 1801.

stud he sired two exceptional colts who surpassed all opposition in the 1850s: *Lexington* and *Lecompte*.

Lexington was foaled in 1850 on Dr Elisha Warfield's horse farm in Kentucky. His dam was the speedy but very nervy Alice Corneal. The early part of his life was spent in the lush paddocks with Alice, and it was not until the autumn of 1853 that he was introduced to the racecourse. Dr Warfield named him Darley and it soon became apparent that this descendant of the Byerley Turk was destined for great things. The speed at which he won his races was noticed by the sporting Richard Ten Broeck, an inveterate and wealthy gambler who did not consider that he was taking any risk in purchasing the colt for $2,500. Ten Broeck changed Darley's name to Lexington and sent him to race in the South. The colt was entered in five races, four of which he won in great style. His only defeat was by Lecompte, also a speedy son of Boston.

Four-mile races were still the norm in those days and in the spring of 1855 Lexington broke the record by nearly seven seconds, covering the distance in 7 minutes 19½ seconds. Then he ran his last race, again against Lecompte, over the Metairie Course for a purse of $6,000. Lexington beat his rival decisively. Lecompte, now worth very little, was shipped to England to stand at stud for the short time until his death.

In the latter part of his racing career, Lexington had maintained his brilliance with great courage, for he was slowly losing his sight. Unaware of his progressive disease, Robert Alexander went to see him with a view to buying him and running him as a six-year-old in England. On his first examination he decided to pay the enormous price of $15,000. He saw a horse of no great beauty, his head being small and unremarkable and his shoulders rather straight. His best features were 'an impressive girth, well sprung ribs, powerful hind quarters and faultless legs'. When someone remarked that the purchase price was far too high, Alexander replied by saying that without doubt he would one day realise a larger sum on a colt sired by Lexington. Imagine the new owner's disappointment when he discovered that the horse he had paid for so dearly would soon be completely blind and would never run in his colours. Unable to race him as planned, he sent him to his Woodburn Farm Stud in Kentucky in 1857.

At that time the farm was well established, with a spread of nearly

Sir Archy, described by his owner and trainer William Ransom Johnson, 'as the best horse I ever ever saw.'

3,000 acres. Its reputation was greatly enhanced by the arrival of a horse of Lexington's calibre, and it was due to him and Alexander that Woodburn dominated racing in America for the next thirty years. Robert Alexander, the third generation to live at the farm, had been educated and spent some time in England, hence his plan to race Lexington there. On returning home in 1851, his father having died ten years previously, he found a flourishing farm, with a racing stable which was practically non-existent. He set about remedying this deficiency, planning to import good bloodstock from Europe. The first British stallion to arrive was *Scythian*. He made little or no impression. Alexander was all set for a return visit to England to find another stallion. However, a friend pointed out the merits of Lexington, then at the height of his brilliance, and a deal was struck with Ten Broeck.

On the farm Robert Alexander took outside mares to board all the year round. He was one of the first major breeders to do so. He issued a catalogue of Woodburn horses every year for thirty years. The first, printed in 1857 states:

> In this establishment mares sent to be bred to the horses belonging to it can be kept for any length of time, from a week to a year at rates from 50 cents to $1.50 according to the kind of care desired. Should any particular treatment be required causing additional trouble or expense, the instructions shall be strictly followed.
>
> For my own convenience in breeding and with a view of giving every facility to those breeders who are disposed to avail themselves of the opportunity here offered, I have purchased the celebrated horse LEXINGTON; and have also imported a young horse SCYTHIAN — both of whom will stand at Woodburn Stud Farm.

Alexander made sure that he knew the pedigree of each mare who came to visit his stallions. Thus he was one of the first breeders, in fact the most important one, to furnish pedigrees for the first American Stud Book, written by Sanders Bruce and published in 1868.

Lexington's first foals were born in 1858 and were of such promise that his reputation was assured. Three years later he became leading sire, a position he maintained for sixteen of the next seventeen years.

2 | The Great Triumvirate

IT WAS IN 1861 that the 'Great Triumvirate', as they were known, were foaled. They were Lexington's best progeny and the most successful to race in the period before the Civil War. Named *Norfolk*, *Kentucky* and *Asteroid*, they triumphed in every race they contested bar one, the Jersey Derby of 1864 in which Kentucky was defeated by Norfolk. Theodore Winters had come from California with the intention of buying *Norfolk*. He was asked $15,001 for the horse and had no hesitation in clinching the deal. Alexander's assertion at the time of Lexington's purchase that he would one day sell a son for more than he had given for the sire proved correct. Winters had a ranch in Yolo County and it was there that the undefeated Norfolk stood, after winning three good races in California from a highly esteemed horse named *Lodi*. The mares brought to him were, by and large, of rather mediocre quality. He never sired an animal who matched his own ability. However, when bred to a mare called Marian he did succeed in siring three top stakes winners, including *Emperor of Norfolk*.

Kentucky, purchased by a group from New York, was comparatively young when he left Woodburn Farm to race on the East Coast. He acquired a formidable reputation and was obliged to carry an extra 10lb in all his races. This was a unique condition and showed in what awe he was held on the racecourse. Brilliant though he was, he failed to pass on these qualities to his progeny, though he did sire eight stakes winners.

Asteroid, Alexander's favourite, was the colt with which he did not part. He was his pride and joy, valued above all the others with the possible exception of Lexington himself. The most handsome of all Lexington's foals, Asteroid proved to be matchless on the racecourse, remaining unbeaten in his twelve starts. It was Alexander's proud boast: 'I think him the best racehorse in the United States by long odds, and if I can keep him well and right I can beat Lexington's time by several seconds under similar circumstances.'

It was planned that the 'Great Triumvirate' should meet for a contest in the summer of 1865. Norfolk was to come east, but for reasons which have never been explained he was pulled out of the race. Then during preparations for the great contest, Asteroid met with an accident which tragically put an end to his racing career. He went to take up stud duties with his sire at the farm where he was foaled.

Asteroid was now four years old, and the Civil War, which had broken out in the year of his foaling, still raged in full fury across the Southern States. By the summer of 1865 it threatened to engulf Woodburn. One evening in October a band of renegades swept down on the farm. In a daring raid they made off with Asteroid and four two-year-olds, all valuable sons of Lexington. Alexander was nearly beside himself. Apart from the loss of a priceless stallion, he was worried about the treatment his favourite would receive. He hastily gathered together as many of his friends from the surrounding countryside as he could and they set off in hot pursuit of the thieves. It was a long, hard and exasperating chase but at last they succeeded in catching up with the raiders. The leader of the band was mounted on Asteroid and at first refused to return him. He averred that he had never had such a superb horse between his knees and he had no intention of parting with him. After a long argument he finally agreed to exchange him for the sum of $250 which would buy him a serviceable hack. The friends returned to the farm relieved to have Asteroid with them.

Alexander was not to be left in peace for long. Shortly afterwards, the stud was raided for a second time. The farm's two prize trotting stallions, Bay Chief and Abdullah, were stolen. Once again connections at the farm

BELOW
Norfolk, oldest of the Great Triumvirate.

OPPOSITE
Kentucky (top) and Asteroid, the other members of the Great Triumvirate.

set off in pursuit of the thieves; but this time they failed to catch them. Instead, after riding for hours they came upon Bay Chief. He had bled to death from a bullet wound. Searching further they discovered Abdullah. He had been ridden into the ground and was dying. They dispatched him to save him from further suffering.

Alexander had not been at the farm when the second raid had taken place. As soon as he heard of it he realised that his stallions would be in constant danger. He surmised that the only reason Lexington had survived unmolested was that he, being very famous, was known to be blind and therefore useless as a soldier's mount. So he decided that, rather than risk another raid, he would take them as far away from trouble as he could. Quickly and quietly he rounded up Lexington, Asteroid and some other horses, took them down to the railroad and loaded them on to a train bound for Illinois. Whether they could remain out of reach of the war there was uncertain. Whether they would ever return to Woodburn, or if indeed Woodburn would still be standing at the end of the war Alexander knew not, but he had made a great effort to keep his prized stallions secure, and for the time being at least they were safe.

This was not his only worry — Illinois was not as renowned for bloodstock as Kentucky. There were few, if any, mares of quality for the stallions to serve. So it was with relief that Alexander, before long, heard of the cessation of hostilities. He still did not know if his farm had survived — so many had been razed to the ground. But to his joy he found that, although in a state of disrepair, it could be made habitable again. Renovation took about a year and already Alexander's health was failing. But before his death in 1867 he lived to see his two stallions grazing in their old paddocks.

Horses were Robert Alexander's passion. He spent his whole life breeding, racing and caring for them. He never married and had no sons to follow him. The farm passed to his younger brother, Alexander John Alexander. This worthy gentleman had little interest in horses. He preferred raising good crops and breeding fine cattle. But he was astute enough to know that the breeding of racehorses on a farm with an excellent reputation was a profitable enterprise. He contacted a relative, Daniel Swigert, and offered him the post of stud manager. Swigert accepted with alacrity and proceeded to build up the stud until its reputation equalled that enjoyed before the Civil War. This largely depended on Lexington because Asteroid, after all his vicissitudes and the efforts made by his owner to keep him safe, proved almost useless as a stallion. Nevertheless, he must have been an engaging character for he inspired great affection in both Robert and Alexander John. The latter kept him as a pet, and he wandered happily in the bluegrass until he died in 1886.

Lexington went from strength to strength, his offspring, about two hundred in all, earning $1,159,000 – a vast sum for the time. However, great though his colts were, it was his daughters who carried on the Diomed line. His most promising son and one of his last foals was *Duke of Magenta*. He won eleven out of twelve races in America and then as a three-year-old boarded ship for England to continue his career. While at sea the Duke became ill and despite devoted attention developed 'roaring'. So before he even landed his racing days were over.

Through Rey del Caredas, Norfolk's grandson, who raced in England under the name of Americus, the Diomed line can be traced through his daughter Americus Girl to Lady Josephine, Lady Juror and Mumtaz Mahal ('Ornament of the Palace', named after the favourite wife of Shah Jahan and for whom he built the Taj Mahal). They lead three important male lines: Fair Trial, Tudor Minstrel and Nasrullah.

Lexington died in 1875 and has been revered by lovers of horse racing from that day to this. *The American Racing Manual* for 1986 records that 'the negligence of American breeders permitted this magnificent male line which began with the first Epsom Derby winner Diomed, and came down through Sir Archy, Timoleon and Boston to Lexington, to become all but extinct. Rey el Tierra, a Rey el Rio foal of 1945, who died in 1964, carried the Lexington strain'. Rey el Tierra sired El Tesoro. Two sons of El Tesoro, who died in the 1980s, have shown little promise. Rey el Carrcra, foaled in 1972, and El Correo, a year younger, are both standing in South Dakota. To date neither has sired a single winner.

Lexington's fame is sung in the nineteenth-century ballad by Hyder Ali:

> Blind he peers about, but sees not,
> Now and then he pricks his ears,
> Lis'ning for the judges' summons,
>   waiting vainly for the cheers
> That were wont of old to greet him
>   when he trod the track a king,
> When met and told each other of
>   his greatness in the ring.
> Whispers fly about the race tracks
>   when some mighty deed is done –
> Tis no more than we expected from the blood of
>   LEXINGTON.

The Tourbillon Line in the USA, Canada and Argentina

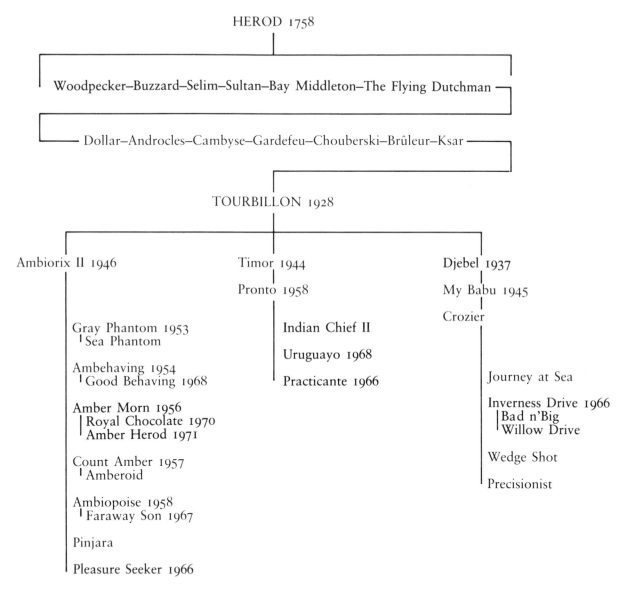

HEROD 1758

Woodpecker–Buzzard–Selim–Sultan–Bay Middleton–The Flying Dutchman

Dollar–Androcles–Cambyse–Gardefeu–Chouberski–Brûleur–Ksar

TOURBILLON 1928

Ambiorix II 1946

Gray Phantom 1953
Sea Phantom

Ambehaving 1954
Good Behaving 1968

Amber Morn 1956
Royal Chocolate 1970
Amber Herod 1971

Count Amber 1957
Amberoid

Ambiopoise 1958
Faraway Son 1967

Pinjara

Pleasure Seeker 1966

Timor 1944

Pronto 1958

Indian Chief II

Uruguayo 1968

Practicante 1966

Djebel 1937

My Babu 1945

Crozier

Journey at Sea

Inverness Drive 1966
Bad n'Big
Willow Drive

Wedge Shot

Precisionist

3 | The Tourbillon Line

THE FLYING DUTCHMAN (foaled in 1846), whose story is told on page 109, was a direct descendant of Herod. He was exported to France and, through his son Dollar, ensured the continuation of the Byerley Turk line, both there and in the USA.

Many years later, when racing in New York had come to a virtual standstill from 1910 to 1913 because of a law prohibiting betting, one of the leading owners in that locality, Herman Duryea by name, decided to take his string of horses to France. This not inconsiderable task accomplished, he set about preparing to race both there and elsewhere in Europe, and planning his breeding programme.

One of the best of his fillies was Frizette by Hamburg. She had proved her worth as a stakes winner in America. Mated with Irish Lad she produced a high class filly named Banshee. As a two-year-old Banshee finished second in the Prix Morny at Deauville and a year later won the French 1,000 Guineas (Poule d'Essai des Pouliches). Duryea had in his stables a powerful stallion named Durbar II. When Banshee finished her racing career it was decided that she should be covered by Durbar. He had won the 1914 Epsom Derby and great things were expected from the union. Their owner was not disappointed when in the fullness of time Banshee produced a promising filly foal.

Subsequently Duryea decided to put some of his stock on the market. It must have been good quality, for a number of horses, including Banshee's filly, now named Durban, were purchased by Marcel Boussac, the leading breeder and owner in France. She proved as speedy as her dam, winning the Championship of France as a two-year-old.

Looking round for a stallion to serve Durban at the end of her racing career, Boussac decided on an outcross whose distance running and staying power would complement her speed. His choice fell on the majestic Ksar, a Classic-winning son of the Dollar line. He had achieved success in the French Derby (Prix du Jockey-Club) and the Prix Royal-Oak (the equivalent of the St Leger) as well as twice winning the Prix de l'Arc de Triomphe. So Durban visited Ksar on two occasions, which resulted in a top racing filly named Diadème and a colt who was to bear the name of *Tourbillon*.

Tourbillon was a precocious colt but possessed neither the looks nor the staying power of his sire. Races run at top speed from start to finish were beyond his capabilities in his third year. If the jockey was able to hold him up in the early stages of the race then, and only then, could the horse produce a burst of speed at the finish. However, before his career started to decline, he did win the 1931 French Derby. On the strength of that he started favourite for the Prix de l'Arc de Triomphe but finished out of the first three. Pearl Cap, the future dam of Pearl Diver, was first, followed by Amfortas, a four-year-old son of Ksar. Prince Rose, who was to become the leading stallion in Belgium, was third.

Tourbillon did not race again. He took up stud duties and became a first class sire. He headed the list of leading French stallions three times, was second three times and third twice. However, little service was paid to the continuance of the Dollar line. Marcel Boussac restricted the number of nominations he allowed to other breeders. Had Tourbillon's seed been scattered more widely it is possible, if not probable, that the dynasty would not have depended on such a narrow range of first class horses.

4 | Ambiorix II, Timor and My Babu

Two sons and a grandson of Tourbillon crossed the Atlantic. They were Ambiorix II, Timor and My Babu by Djebel. *Ambiorix II* was foaled in 1946. He was a dark bay colt out of Lavendula, of the Sweet Lavender branch. He was the last of Tourbillon's top class colts. His sire was eighteen years old and his dam sixteen when he was foaled. In line with French policy, he was lightly raced at two. He won the Selsey Maiden Stakes and on his third racecourse appearance following that success he started favourite in the one-mile Grand Critérium at Longchamp in October. His two-length victory established him as a top class two year old.

In his third year he ran four times, winning twice and twice finishing second. His successes were in the Prix Greffulhe and the Prix Lupin both over ten and a half furlongs. The mile-and-a-half Prix Hocquart proved a severe test of stamina for him, as did the French Derby. He failed to catch the leader on each occasion. This leaning towards speed rather than stamina, though disappointing for Boussac, was judged to be more suitable for the American style of racing. When Mr A.B. Hancock Jnr. offered $250,000 for Ambiorix, the bid was accepted and the horse went to stand at Claiborne Farm in Paris, Kentucky.

This family concern was a very prestigious establishment. Mr Hancock had wished to buy My Babu but the price had not been within his range. As it was, Ambiorix served him well. He headed the American sire list in 1961 and was responsible for fifty-one stakes winners. However, his line has never been as strong in America as that of Nasrullah, whose forebears, both male and female, were noted for speed. Much emphasis is placed on this type of racehorse, which is well suited to the American style of racing.

The daughters of Ambiorix have had some influence, particularly the brilliant High Voltage, champion filly of 1954. His mares have produced fifty-two stakes winners, including Ragusa, a Classic winner and top class stallion in Europe. Ambiorix died in 1975, aged twenty-nine, while enjoying his well-earned retirement at Claiborne Farm.

Of his sons, *Ambiopoise* has sired only one truly Classic colt in *Faraway Son*. But another son, Twice Worthy, won a Group 1 race in

1971, the Suburban Handicap at Belmont Park. *Ambiopoise*, foaled in 1958, was the bay son of Bull Poise by Bull Lea. He was a stakes winner of ten races from the ages of two to four, and at stud was among the leading stallions, siring ten stakes winners.

Faraway Son, foaled in 1967 out of a brown mare named Locust Time by Spy Song, was a dark bay or brown horse standing 16hh. At two he won the Critérium de Maisons Laffitte, a maiden race at Chantilly, came second in the Prix de la Forêt and third in the Grand Critérium. At three he finished second in both the Prix du Moulin de Longchamp and the Prix de Fontainebleau and was third in the French 2,000 Guineas (Poule d'Essai des Poulains). At four he raced in France and England. He became Champion Miler in France, with successes in the Prix du Moulin de Longchamp (Gr.1)*, the Prix de la Porte Maillot (Gr.3), the Prix de la Jonchère (Gr.3) and the Prix du Rond-Point (Gr.3). He came second in the Sussex Stakes and the Grand Prix d'Evry (Gr.2). He went to stud in 1971 and was among the leading sires in France in 1977. In 1985, standing at Gainesway Farm in Kentucky, he commanded a fee of $5,000. He had up to that time sired seventeen stakes winners of whom the best was the mare *Waya*. She had fourteen wins, including four Group 1 races, between the ages of two and five and became Champion Older Mare.

Other sons include Boitron (Fr.), Bynoderm, My Best and Prospero, but none of these has won a Group 1 race.

Ambehaving, a brown colt out of Dentifrice by Reaping Reward was foaled in 1954. He was a stakes winner of $159,838 and sire of twenty-three stakes winners. His son *Good Behaving* out of Miss Cor, a chestnut mare by Correlation, was standing in the late 1980s at Nickels and Dimes Farm, Libertyville, Illinois. A 16hh chestnut, foaled in 1968, Good Behaving was a stakes winner of $159,838 and has sired twelve winners of over $5 million, as well as winners in Puerto Rico and Belgium.

Count Amber was a bay foaled in 1957 out of Dorrine B by Crafty Admiral. He was a stakes winner of six races. His progeny included Amberoid, Amber Moon, Gray Phantom, Pleasure Seeker and Pinjara. *Amberoid* won the mile-and-a-half Belmont Stakes in 1966. The dark bay *Amber Morn* out of Break O'Morn by Eight Thirty was foaled in 1956 and raced for five seasons. At four he won the Bowling Green Handicap over a mile and a half on turf in the record time of 2 minutes 29.2 seconds. Two of his progeny won the Canadian Queen's Plate Stakes (Gr.1) at Woodbine Kentucky†. They were *Royal Chocolate* (1973) and *Amber Herod* (1974).

Gray Phantom, a grey like his dam Grey Flight by Mahmoud, was

* The official Pattern Race classifications were introduced in England, France and Ireland in 1971, and in Germany and Italy a year later.

† The official Pattern Race classifications were introduced in the USA in 1973.

foaled in 1953. He was a stakes winner of sixteen races worth $130,830. His son *Sea Phantom*, out of Sea Caprice by Pearl Orient, won $82,309 and retired to stud in 1976, having won twelve races. The bay colt *Pleasure Seeker*, foaled in 1966, was out of Troublepeg by Mr Trouble by Mahmoud. His chief victories were the Labour Day Handicap (1969) as a three-year-old, and the 1970 Hollywood Gold Cup (Gr.1). Altogether he earned $211,297. He retired to stud in 1971. By 1986 he had sired six stakes winners. Their total earnings, excluding those in Mexico, amounted to $1,832,041.

The big bay *Pinjara*, foaled in 1965, was out of Banri an Oir by Royal Charger. He did not make much impression as a two-year-old but at three he won five times. His victories included the nine-furlong Cinema Handicap, the Cabrillo Handicap over a mile and the El Dorado Handicap, also over a mile. At four years he won three times, including the

Ambiorix II.

Claiborne Farm at Paris in the bluegrass country of Kentucky, where Ambiorix stood at stud.

Present-day photograph of mares in the paddock at Claiborne Farm.

Century Handicap and the San Bernardino Handicap in which he carried top weight. In the Sierra Madre Handicap, Indulto beat him by a nose. At five he had three successes, the most important being the Coronado Stakes. In his final year of racing he won five times, including the Del Mar Handicap, again carrying top weight, the Crenshaw Stakes and Sierra Madre Handicap. He retired to the Westerly Stud Farms, Santa Ynez, California in 1970.

Other winners by Ambiorix include *Pelegrin*, San Marino Handicap (L.); *Amri-An*, Del Mar Debutante Stakes (Gr.2) and *Kerry Bay*, winner of $16,805 as a three-year-old.

Timor, a chestnut by Tourbillon out of Samya by Nimbus, son of Nearco, was born in 1944. He raced in France, where he won valuable stakes races, including the Prix Hocquart. Exported to stud in Argentina, he sired a colt of some importance named *Pronto*, a bay out of Prosperina by Gusty. The mare was a great grand-daughter of Mumtaz Mahal. Pronto, foaled in 1958, was unraced at two but won all his three starts the following year. Having made a successful racecourse debut, something which earned him much kudos, he won the Gran Premio Internacional Organizacion Sudamericana de Fomento del Pura Sangre de Carrera over a mile at Palermo, Argentina, and later in the season had an easy victory in the mile-and-a-half Premio Miguel Alfredo Martinez de Hoz, at San Isidro. He was ranked among the best of his generation and hopes for his further success were high. But it was not to be. He suffered an injury which put him out of racing altogether. He retired to stud having earned nearly 1½ million Pesos.

Pronto sired *Practicante*, *Indian Chief II* and *Uruguayo*, all three of whom became Champion three-year-old and Horse of the Year in Argentina, and *Uruguayana*, Champion Sprinter of Argentina. His American Stakes winners include *Tuqui II* (San Marcos Handicap, Santa Anita), *Red Top III* (Del Mar Handicap), *Hello Theo* (Visitation Stakes) and *Primed* (Larkspur Stakes, Probationers' Stakes).

Pronto's progeny won over an average distance of seven and a half furlongs. He was imported to North America in 1969 where he stood at Claiborne Farm, Kentucky. He was then sold and syndicated, residing at Shoshone Farm in Florida. In 1976 they had a dispersal sale and he was bought by the Fasig-Tipton Company, Elmont, New York.

My Babu was sold for export to the United States in 1956. On his arrival he was syndicated for $600,000 and immediately went to stud. He was leading sire of two-year-olds with his first crop. He sired *Crozier*, Ginger Fizz, Green Hornet, Pack Trip, Fusilier Boy, Garwol and Bronze Babu, all of whom were stakes winners.

Crozier was foaled in 1958 out of Miss Olympia by Olympia, a grandson of Hyperion. At two he won the Prairie State Stakes and the Washington Park Futurity; at three he won the Derby Trial and Hibiscus Stakes, and was second in the Kentucky Derby (Gr.1), the Jersey Derby, the Flamingo Stakes, the Fountain of Youth Stakes and the Florida Derby (Gr.1); at four he won the Aqueduct Stakes and the Palos Verdes Handicap and at five the Santa Anita Handicap (Gr.1), the Bernardino Handicap and the San Carlos Handicap. He retired from racing at the end of the 1963 season having earned $641,733. In 1976, standing at Hooper Farms, Ocala, Florida, he commanded a fee of $5,000. His stakes winning progeny include *Inverness Drive*, *Beat Inflation*, *Wedge Shot*, *Precisionist*, *Pitching Wedge*, *Admiral's Shield*, *Fenicia* and *Journey at Sea*.

Inverness Drive, a bay horse standing 15.3hh, was foaled in 1966 out of Martial Maiden by Court Martial. He raced for five seasons, earning

$124,880. He won the Graduation Stakes as a two-year-old, the Santa Catalina Stakes at three, was second in the Meteor Handicap at four and as a five-year-old won the Sacramento Handicap and finished second in the Los Angeles Handicap. At stud he produced winners of 607 races worth $6,098,481 from 1973 to 1986. They include *Bad n' Big, Willow Drive* and *Pillager. Bad n' Big* had 13 wins including three Group 2 races, the Cinema Handicap, the Golden Gate Handicap and the Longacres Mile, and the Caballero Handicap (a listed race), plus the Group 3 El Dorado Handicap and the Bing Crosby Handicap. *Willow Drive* was successful in the Bashford Manor Stakes and finished second in the Group 1 Sapling Stakes.

The chesnut *Beat Inflation*, foaled in 1973 out of Teacher's Art by Quibu, did not run as a two-year-old and had three minor successes at three. At four he won the Group 3 Los Angeles Handicap at Hollywood and the Hollywood Express Handicap, both races under a mile, and was second in the Première Handicap (Gr.3) and the Lakes and Flowers Handicap, also at Hollywood. He stayed in training for another two seasons but had little success and retired to stud as a six-year-old with total winnings to his credit of $151,220. His foals from 1980 to 1986 won 203 races worth $1,583,590. They include Blonde Inflation, Inflation Beater, Jerry F and Inflation Vacation.

Of Crozier's other stakes-winning progeny, *Wedge Shot* won the Futurity Stakes (Gr.1), was second in the Sapling Stakes (Gr.1) and won the Baldwin Stakes (Group 3). *Precisionist* won seventeen times from two to five years. He was Champion Sprinter, winning the Breeders' Cup Sprint Stakes, the Charles H. Strub Stakes, the Californian Stakes and the Woodward Stakes (all Gr.1). *Pitching Wedge* won the Florida Breeders' Handicap, and *Admiral's Shield* the Derby Trial Stakes. *Fenicia* won the 1975 Clasico Malinche Stakes Jockey Club Mexicano in Mexico and became Champion Three-year-old Filly and Champion Older Mare. *Journey at Sea*'s eight wins included the Swaps Stakes (Gr.1).

The Dynasty is not very strongly represented in America, but *Crested Wave* by Crozier reached number five in the 1987 Leading Stallion Register of Australia.

PART FOUR

The Highflyer Line

The Highflyer Line

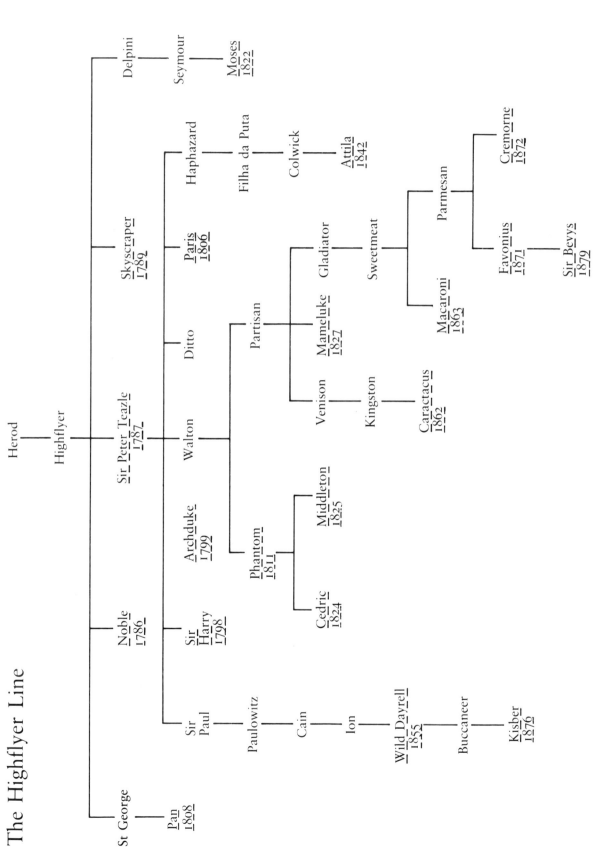

Derby winners and date of win underlined

Derby Winners of The Highflyer Line

Year	Horse	Jockey	Owner	Colours	Exported to
1786	Noble (B)	Sam Arnull	Mr T Panton	Buff	
1787	Sir Peter Teazle (Br)	Sam Arnull	12th Earl of Derby	1780 green & white stripe	
1789	Skyscraper (B)	Sam Chifney	5th Duke of Bedford	1788 black, white cap	
1798	Sir Harry (Br)	Sam Arnull	Mr J. Cookson	Purple & white stripe	USA
1799	Archduke (Br)	John Arnull	Sir F. Standish	Purple & straw-coloured	USA
1803	Ditto (B)	Bill Clift	Sir H. Williamson	Mazarin blue, white cap	
1806	Paris (Br)	John Shepherd	3rd Baron Foley	Straw, black cap	
				Green & white stripe, same cap	
1808	Pan (Ch)	Frank Collinson	Sir H. Williamson	Straw, black cap	
1811	Phantom (B)	Frank Buckle	Sir J. Shelley	Black, white cap	
1822	Moses (B)	Tom Goodison	H.R.H. Duke of York	Purple, black cap	
1824	Cedric (Ch)	Tom Robinson	Sir John Shelley	Black, white cap	
1825	Middleton (Ch)	Tom Robinson	5th Earl of Jersey	Dark blue, white stripe, black cap	
1827	Mameluke (B)	Tom Robinson	5th Earl of Jersey	ditto	Russia
1842	Attila (B)	Bill Scott	Sir G. Anson	1838 red, blue sleeves, white cap, later all white	USA maybe
1855	Wild Dayrell (Br)	Robert Sherwood	Mr F. Popham	White, green and red sleeves and cap	Germany
1862	Caractacus (B)	John Parsons	Mr Snewing	Light blue, white cap	
1863	Macaroni (B)	Thomas Chaloner	Mr R. C. Naylor	Primrose, cherry cap	
1871	Favonius (Ch)	Thomas French	Baron M. de Rothschild	Dark blue, yellow cap	Died en route
1872	Cremorne (B)	Charles Maidment	Capt. H. Savile	Yellow, scarlet cap, gold tassel	
1876	Kisber (B)	Charles Maidment	Mr A. Baltazzi	French grey, scarlet cap	
1879	Sir Bevys (Br)	George Fordham	Baron L. de Rothschild	Dark blue, yellow cap	Germany

B=Bay   Br=Brown   Ch=Chesnut

The entry for Highflyer in *William Pick's Racing Calendar*.

HIGHFLYER, the property of Mr. *Tattersall*, was got by Herod; his dam, (Marc Antony's dam) by Blank; grandam by Regulus, a daughter of Soreheels, (which mare was the dam of Matchless, South, and Danby Cade); a daughter of Makeless, and was Sir Ralph Milbank's famous black mare, the dam of Hartley's Blind Horse. At Newmarket second October Meeting, 1777, HIGHFLYER won a sweepstakes of 900gs. for three-year olds, colts 8ft. fillies 7ft. 11lb. D. I. beating Justice, Bourdeaux, Sweetmarjoram, &c. In the second Spring Meeting, 1778, *Highflyer* won a sweepstakes of 2600gs. for four-year olds, colts 8ft. fillies 7ft. 11lb. B. C. beating Il'mio, Thunderbolt, Jupiter, Chesfield, Fulmine, and four others. In the July Meeting, *Highflyer* won a sweepstakes of 600gs. colts 8ft. 7lb. fillies 8ft. 4lb. B. C. beating Stormer, Satellite, and Dragon. In the first October Meeting, he won the renewed 1400gs. colts 8ft. 10lb. fillies 8ft. 7lb. B. C. beating Il'mio, Firm, and Jupiter; he also won the weights and scales plate of 100gs. wt. for age, B. C. beating Pearl, Vestal, and Tremamondo. In the second October Meeting, he received 400gs. forfeit in a post sweepstakes. In the Houghton Meeting, *Highflyer* at 8ft. beat Lord Clermont's Dictator, five years old, 8ft. 7lb. B. C. 500gs. In the first Spring Meeting, 1779, *Highflyer* at 8ft. 3lb. won a sweepstakes of 750gs. B. C. beating Mr. Stapleton's Magog, 8ft. 7lb. In the second Spring Meeting, he won a sweepstakes of 700gs. 8ft. 7lb. each, B. C. beating Dorimant, aged, and Dictator, six years old. He afterwards walk'd over for a subscription of 280gs. at Nottingham, and the great subscription of 295l. at York; he also won the great subscription of 295l. for six-year olds and aged horses, at York. He likewise won the King's plate at Lichfield, beating, at two heats, (though lame) Lord Grosvenor's bay mare, by Dux, and Mr. Smallman's Chesfield. *Highflyer* was never beat, nor ever paid a forfeit, and is undoubtedly the best horse of his time in England. The sums he won and received amounts to 8920gs. though he never started after *five years old*. HIGHFLYER is now a stallion, and is sire of his Royal Highness the Prince of Wales's ROCKINGHAM, (late *Camden*) who has proved himself to be much superior, in point of running, to any other horse in England: He is also sire of Lord Derby's *Lady Teazel*, Mr. Bullock's *Miss Blanchard*, Mr. Coates's *Omphale*, Mr. Goodrick's *Dexter*, Mr. Hutchinson's *Fairy*, Sir Frank Standish's *Delpini*, Mr. Bullock's *Balloon*, &c.

Highflyer was a bay colt bred by Sir Charles Bunbury out of a mare named Rachel, by Blank, a Godolphin stallion. He was foaled in a field where some highflyer walnut trees grew*, and was named by Lord Bolingbroke who bought him from Sir Charles. He was re-sold in 1779 to Richard Tattersall of the auctioneering firm. Highflyer was the outstanding racehorse of his time, winning £8,920 in his unbeaten career. He sired three Derby winners: Noble, *Sir Peter Teazle* and Skyscraper.

* These walnut trees were introduced into England from Persia and India early in the eighteenth century. They grew to a height of about 60 feet, which may account for the name 'highflyer'.

TRENTHAM, see page 390.

———— ————

TRUMPATOR, at 5gs a mare, and 5s. to the groom, at Chippenham, near Newmarket.

N. B. Only two of his get have started, and both won at Newmarket.

The money to be paid before the mares are taken away.

———— ————

VERTUMNUS, see page 379.

VOLUNTEER, see page 378.

———— ————

At Petworth, in Suffex,

WOODPECKER, } at 20gs a mare, and one guinea
MERCURY, } the groom.
ASSASSIN, } at 2gs a mare, and half a guinea
TRENTHAM, } the groom.

The money to be paid before the mares are taken away.

———— ————

YOUNG HIGHFLYER will cover 60 mares, and no more, at 3gs a mare, and 5s. the groom, at Croke's Repofitory, Briftol.

Young Highflyer was got by Highflyer, he is own brother to the famous Maid of all Work, Cowflip, Mifs Blanchard, &c. &c. His dam is own fifter to that celebrated racer, Tandem, got by Syphon; his grand dam by Regulus, his great grand

grand dam by Snip, his great great grand dam by Cottingham, fon of Hartley's Blind Horfe; his great great great grand dam called the Warlock Galloway, and was the dam of Mr. Routh's Cub, and Black Eyes, and grand dam of Judgement and Apollo, by Lifter's Snake, a daughter of the Bald Galloway, a daughter of the Carlifle Turk, fire of the Carlifle gelding's dam, and out of a daughter of the Pulleine old Arabian, &c.

Young Highflyer is as high-bred a horfe as any in the kingdom, as is to be obferved, his 1ft, 2d, 3d, and 4th fires, Highflyer, King Herod, Old Tartar, and Partner; his dams, Syphon, Regulus, Snip, and Hartley's blind Horfe; and were fons and grandfons of the Godolphin and Darley Arabians.

Young Highflyer is 16 hands one inch high, juftly proportioned, great finew, short legged, and is calculated to get racers, hunters, or coach horfes.

———— ————

YOUNG PUMPKIN, see page 374.

The advertisement for Highflyer in *James Weatherby's Racing Calendar*, 1791.

HERE LIETH
The perfect and beautiful symmetry
Of the much lamented
HIGHFLYER;
By whom, and his wonderful offspring,
The celebrated TATTERSALL acquired a noble
fortune,
But was not ashamed to acknowledge it.
In gratitude to this famous
STALLION,
He call'd an elegant mansion he built
HIGHFLYER HALL.
At these extensive demesnes
It is not unusual for some of the
Highest characters
To regale sumptuously,
When they do the owner the honor
Of accepting his hospitality.
A gentleman of the Turf,
Tho' he has no produce from the above
STALLION,
Begs leave to pay this small tribute
To his memory

Epitaph for Highflyer from *Pierce Egan's Book of Sports*, 1832.

1 | Sir Peter Teazle

OPPOSITE
Richard Tattersall by
Thomas Beach, 1787. A
painting of Highflyer
and Highflyer Hall can
be seen behind him.

IN 1787 THE 12th Earl of Derby succeeded in winning the race named after him with his home-bred colt, Sir Peter Teazle. By Highflyer out of Papillon by Snap, he was named as a compliment to the Earl's second wife, Miss Ellen Farren. Her reputation as an actress had been greatly enhanced by her portrayal of Lady Teazle in Sheridan's *School for Scandal*. He was foaled at the family seat at Knowsley, in Lancashire, where his high-walled paddock can still be seen. He was a magnificent animal, standing some 16hh when fully grown, with good shoulders and very powerful quarters.

He made his racecourse debut in the Derby, beating Gunpowder by Eclipse, and Bustler by Florizel. In the same year he won a sweepstake at Ascot, a 1,400 guineas Subscription Purse at Newmarket and the Prince of Wales' Plate two days later. In fact, he completed his three-year-old season without a single defeat. In 1788 he remained unbeaten until the First October Meeting. Here he was matched with the Duke of Queensberry's Dash, by Florizel, with a handicap of 35lb. He failed to beat Dash, but later beat the Duke of Bedford's Maria, though the odds were once more against him.

The following year he arrived fresh and apparently fit at the Craven Meeting, where he won the Subscription Stakes from the talented Meteor and Gunpowder. But all was not right with him. He was unable to meet a challenge from Dash to a six mile race for 1,000 guineas. The following October he broke down while taking part in a match with the Duke of Queensberry's Mulberry, to whom he was giving 28lb.

Sir Peter was therefore retired to stud where he proceeded to prove his worth as a stallion. He was the sire of four Derby winners: *Sir Harry* (1798), *Archduke* (1799), *Ditto* (1803) and *Paris* (1806); two winners of the Oaks: *Hermione* (1794) and *Parisot* (1796), and four winners of the St Leger: *Ambrosio* (1796), *Fyldner* (1806), *Paulina* (1807) and *Petronius* (1808). Lord Derby was at one point offered 7,000 guineas for him by some gentlemen from America. He promptly refused, with this remark: 'Had I been disposed to part with Sir Peter, I could have had 10,000 guineas for him.' So Sir Peter stayed at Knowsley. When he died he was buried close to the boxes. A plain stone, carved simply with the words 'Sir Peter' marks where he lies.

Edward Smith-Stanley, Twelfth Earl of Derby, owner of Sir Peter Teazle and founder of the Derby.

In spite of the Derby family's continued and generous support of racing, it was not until 1924 that their colours were again carried to victory in the Derby. Sansovino won by six lengths in what was a veritable quagmire. But sixteen Derby winners trace their descent from Sir Peter. All sixteen colts are worthy of note, the following being of particular interest.

Middleton, a chesnut colt by Phantom out of Web, was foaled in 1822 and owned by the fifth Earl of Jersey. He was a big, ungainly animal, clumsy in his movements. He was reckoned to be of so little promise that he was not raced as a juvenile. However, by the time he reached three he had improved sufficiently to be entered for his first race – the Derby.

The morning of the race dawned and his lad was despatched with a bucket of water for use in the plaiting of Middleton's mane. This reprobate, previously bribed, allowed the horse to drink the water. When the head lad arrived to check on progress he found a very full horse and a very empty bucket. Panic reigned, until the arrival of the trainer. Edwards had dealt with relatives of Middleton before and assured the head lad that Middleton would win. What happened to the lad history does not tell, but the colt was walked the four miles to the race and, with Jem Robinson up, won at 7–4.

Plagued by navicular disease, he never ran again. He was retired to stud at the Horse Bazaar, King Street, Portman Square, and was exported to Russia in 1833.

Mameluke was a bay colt by Partisan out of Miss Sophia. Foaled in 1824, he was named after the famous Turkoman warriors who ruled in Cairo in the fifteenth century. He was bred by Mr R.C. Elwes, and became another Derby winner for the fifth Earl of Jersey. This highly successful owner/breeder won the Derby three times, the 2,000 Guineas twice and the Oaks once. He was fortunate to have in his stables a remarkable mare called Web and an incomparable trainer of Web stock in James Edwards. Mameluke was his only Classic winner out of a dam from another family.

Sir Peter Teazle, by Charles Towne, 1791.

The Earl was appointed Lord Chamberlain of the Household to William IV, and subsequently became Master of the Horse to the young Queen Victoria.

In 1827 he had two runners in the Epsom Classic – Mameluke and Glenartney. The latter started favourite at 5–1, with Mameluke at 9–1. The Earl stated no preference for either colt. Mameluke, with Robinson up, won by two lengths. It was noted that Glenartney had not been ridden out. Rumour had it that this victory suited the Earl and his friends very well – later the winner was sold for £4,000, but an offer of £5,000 was refused for Glenartney. Be that as it may, no proof of the Earl's implication came to light. It was known, however, that Glenartney's jockey, Harry Edwards, had backed Mameluke very heavily. He was a genial, one-eyed scallywag, with great ability but few scruples. He thoroughly

Mameluke at Newmarket, painted by Benjamin Marshall in 1828.

enjoyed turning the tables on the 'swells'. So draw what inference you will.

Attila was a bay colt by Colwick, foaled in the year that Queen Victoria came to the throne. His owner, General the Hon Sir George Anson (1797–1857), was rather more famous than his colt, whom he named after Attila the Hun, the scourge of Europe in the seventh century and a formidable warrior. The General had fought at Waterloo as an ensign in the Foot Guards. He was well regarded both as a sportsman and a tactful and sophisticated man of the world.

Attila was bought for £120, and was sent to be trained by John Scott. This worthy trainer was noted for his generous hospitality, which he extended to the gentry and also the country folk from the East Yorkshire villages around Malton. He must have done his work well, for Attila, with Bill Scott up, won the Derby in 1842. He was then exported to Germany but died en route. Much to his friends' surprise, the General sailed for India in 1853 to become Commander-in-Chief of the British forces there. Had he not been so careful to preserve the etiquette of his dinner table he might have gained valuable time at the start of the Sepoy mutiny, an uprising by native soldiers against their white commanders, brought about by lack of understanding of intrinsic religious differences. Out of respect for his guests the General delayed opening the fateful telegram bringing news of the uprising. Like so many of his compatriots he caught and succumbed to cholera not long after.

There is a bizarre story behind the name *Wild Dayrell*, a colt who lived at Littlecote, near Hungerford, in the county of Berkshire. On a dark, wild night in 1575, Mother Barnes was settling down by the warm hearth in her cottage when she heard knocking on the door. Wondering who could be abroad on such a night, she answered it to find two men seeking her services. She was a midwife. It seemed strange when they insisted on her wearing a blindfold, but she agreed to go with them. On arrival she discovered that her patient was masked and already in labour. She assisted in the delivery, but as soon as the child was born a man of 'ferocious appearance' hurried forward and seized the baby. To Mother Barnes' horror and in spite of her agonised pleas he threw it into the fire and ground it into the glowing embers with his boot.

A handsome bribe was paid for the midwife's silence, but her part in the affair weighed heavily on her conscience. After a time she could keep silent no longer. She reported the murder to a magistrate, bringing as evidence a small piece of tapestry which she had surreptitiously cut from the bed hangings. Suspicion fell on the owner of Littlecote, Wild William Darrell (or Dayrell). His guilt was confirmed by the small fragment which matched the hole in the tapestry curtains. It is said that he escaped with his life by transferring the deeds of the house to Sir John Popham, who was later to become a judge. Dayrell was killed when his horse shied for no apparent reason – on hearing a ghostly baby scream, some said.

Littlecote stayed in the Popham family, and some 277 years later the colt to be named Wild Dayrell was foaled. Francis Popham was a country squire of some means. He dabbled in many forms of sport and owned a mare called Lady Flora. He conceived the notion that he would like to breed a racehorse. This he set about in the style of an enthusiastic amateur. Taking the advice of his stud groom, a man named Rickaby, he bought Ellen Middleton by Bay Middleton from Lord Zetland for the sum of £50. So convinced was the groom of her breeding and worth that she was purchased unseen.

As there was no stallion in the vicinity who matched Mr Popham's requirements, Rickaby was sent to explore further afield. He finally arrived at Barrow's of Newmarket, where he chose Ion, second in the Derby, as the potential sire. Ellen and Lady Flora were duly sent to Newmarket.

So great was their interest and anxiety, that Mr Popham and his groom sat up with Ellen for more than a fortnight before she foaled. On the night of the birth, Francis Popham repaired to the stable to resume his vigil, and soon after midnight the mare produced a colt. The butler was summoned and arrived complete with nightcap bearing wine on a salver for the celebration. Having toasted the small bearer of their hopes, it was decided to move him to a warmer box. A wheelbarrow was brought and the colt carefully installed, to be wheeled by an insistent butler determined to 'wheel the winner of the Derby once in my life'.

At five o'clock that morning, in April 1852, Rickaby was making his way thankfully homeward, when he saw the unusual sight of a pair of wild duck perched on a quick-set hedge beside the road. He was not sure whether this portent boded good or ill for the colt, but he was convinced that there was something fateful in store for him.

Lady Flora had also foaled and the intention was for the filly in due course to go into training with the colt. But Rickaby had never trained a Thoroughbred colt before and since Mr Popham was also at a loss to know what to do with him, he advertised both Wild Dayrell and Creusa, the filly, for sale. Lord Henry Lennox paid 500 guineas for the pair but the colt proved so backward that they were both put up for sale again. As it turned out, Lord Henry would have done well to exercise a little patience. Francis Popham, then in Scotland, sent instructions for them to be bought back and he sold a half-share of the colt to his friend Lord Craven. So back they went to Littlecote Park.

Their early training proceeded in a somewhat countrified style, on a measured two-mile gallop along the river Kennet. During the winter Rickaby would be seen leading the gallops on a five-year-old gelding called Zegra, with his sons following on *Wild Dayrell* and *Creusa*. Come May, the Rickabys moved to Lord Craven's stables at Ashdown with the colt and filly and a couple more horses, where training continued in a more conventional fashion. They had no yardstick to gauge the colt's potential, because he had been matched only with *Zegra*, but he did win one race at Newmarket very easily.

By his third year *Wild Dayrell* had grown to 16½hh and training for the Derby began in earnest. A fast horse called *Lord Albemarle* was brought to gallop with him, but *Wild Dayrell* showed who was master, kicking his heels so high in the air that Robert Sherwood, the jockey engaged to partner him, and his lad had hard work staying in the saddle. Another horse, *Jack Shephard*, was bought at Lincoln for 1,600 guineas and joined the stable, now guarded by Rickaby and two dogs. But *Wild Dayrell* made short work of him. Then *Gamelad* was hired to join in the trial, which took place ten days before the Derby. At six o'clock that morning Lord Craven and his party, which included Francis Popham, assembled on the Weathercock Hill. *Wild Dayrell* wore down all the opposition. Charlton, who rode *Gamelad*, reported, 'I never rode against such a horse as this before.'

The colt's fame spread, but although he was heavily backed the odds did not shorten. Popham became suspicious. He heard rumours that there was a plot against the horse. He sacked the only man in the stables who could have been guilty of complicity. Then he was approached by someone offering him £5,000 if he would withdraw *Wild Dayrell*. This he flatly refused to do. He was determined to make sure that his colt arrived safely at the racecourse. *Wild Dayrell* was due to travel to Epsom in a horse-drawn van. As a precaution, a bullock was substituted and the van driven past Popham. As he suspected, the vehicle had been tampered with. The wheels of the van collapsed and the unfortunate bullock sustained a broken leg.

When the gang who had tried to prevent *Wild Dayrell* from running realised that their plot had failed, they proceeded to back him against their former fancy, *Kingstown*, owned by a villainous bookmaker. *Wild Dayrell* started the race at even money and romped home, a comfortable winner. Francis Popham won £10,000 in bets, but declared that he never wanted to own another Derby winner. And he never did!

Caused, perhaps, by the hard state of the ground, or his running into a quick-set hedge in the paddock, the colt began to have trouble in his near foreleg. Shortly afterwards the other foreleg filled up. Rickaby managed to patch him up to win the Ebor St Leger, but he broke down at Doncaster and was retired to stud. He had little success as a sire. A colt out of Alice Hawthorn died when young, and another colt, The Rake, who was a Derby hope, broke a blood vessel in his final training. It was left to his mouse-brown son Buccaneer to carry on his line. Buccaneer became champion sire in 1868 and his son *Kisber* was three times champion sire in Germany.

Caractacus, bred at Mr Blenkiron's Middle Park Stud, by Kingston out of Defenceless, was a bay colt. He was sold as a yearling in 1860 to the trainer William Day on behalf of Mr Snewing, a publican from Tottenham Court Road. The following spring he went to Zachary's stables at Harpenden, Hertfordshire, where his training was undertaken by one Bob Smith. Named Caractacus after the noble and dignified King of the Silures who, captured and in chains, won the respect of the Emperor Claudius, the colt presented a somewhat different picture. According to one racegoer visiting the paddock at Epsom, he was 'a short legged, powerful trussy horse' – big and above himself.

As a two-year-old he ran three times against very moderate horses and lost each time. Then Bob Smith set out to prepare him for the Derby in a most unusual fashion. He entered him in the Two-and-a-Quarter-mile Great Metropolitan Handicap at Epsom, where the colt was beaten by a head. Mr Snewing was offered £3,000 for him there and then, so he

The earliest known photograph of a race-horse: Wild Dayrell after winning the Derby in 1855.

must have impressed. His owner stated his terms of sale as '£10,000 and an annuity of £100 for my trainer'. The prospective purchaser declined and Caractacus ran three more races over two miles. He was unplaced in the Chester Cup, third in the Northern Handicap at York, and won the Somersetshire Stakes at Bath.

Added to this, he was subjected to some hard gallops on Harpenden racecourse. However, all this work seemed to do him no harm and he turned up on Derby Day looking a good prospect. Not that the racing public took much interest in him – they preferred Mr Snewing's other colt, Spite. The regular jockey, Goater, also spurned Caractacus and elected to ride Spite.

It was left to a sixteen-year-old lad called John Parsons to ride the 40–1 colt. Very slight and a complete novice on the racetrack, he possessed the distinct advantage of knowing his horse. Used to riding him in training, he understood the colt and Caractacus was used to him. Parsons was confident that they could win and calmly set about doing just that. Caractacus came home a neck ahead of Marquis, the favourite. It was a disappointing race for Goater because Spite broke down. Mr Snewing had promised an annuity of £100 to the winner. Bob Smith did well out of it, but promptly lost it all to the bookmakers. Mr Snewing won £20,000 and organised a fête for the poor of Watford, gratefully assisted by sundry clergy.

In spite of being the youngest jockey to win the Derby, Parsons did not pursue a career on the turf. He disappeared and was forgotten by the racing fraternity. Caractacus broke down while being prepared for the St Leger and never raced again. He was not a success at stud.

How *Macaroni* was once the toast of Newmarket is an oft repeated story. His sire Sweetmeat, who changed hands as a foal for 20 guineas, was bought by a Mr Cookson for 300 guineas after he broke down and sold again for 800 guineas. He was an attractive horse of medium build with a 'clever straight head and neck'. Shortly after arriving at Neasham Hall to stand at stud he went blind.

Macaroni, a bay colt out of Jocose by Pantaloon, was foaled in 1860 at the Marquis of Eaton's stud at Eaton. The following year the stables suffered an attack of infectious strangles. Six yearlings, including Macaroni, were so badly affected that it took them a long time to recover. It was decided to sell them all as soon as possible. At about this time Mr R.C. Naylor, a one-time banker from Liverpool, was preparing to set up a stud at Hooton Park. The stud grooms from Eaton and Hooton Park were friendly and the one from Eaton Hall suggested a package deal. So the six yearlings became the property of Mr Naylor for £700. A very good deal it was to prove for, although one died, the other five all won races.

The yearlings were sent to Palace House, Newmarket, to be trained by

James Godding. At that time it was very unfashionable to send horses to Newmarket. It was considered that the going on the Heath was too firm by the summer. Most of the large stables were centred on the Downs in Sussex and Berkshire, where the turf was springy. Newmarket badly needed a Classic victory to restore its fortunes.

Nothing deterred, Godding was confident that he could train winners, even a Derby winner, on the Heath. He set about proving it with his five backward yearlings. Of the five, Carnival was judged to be the best. Macaroni did not run until the autumn, when he came second in a two-horse race on the Abingdon mile.

Betting for the Derby favoured Carnival, but Mr Naylor preferred Macaroni. He showed his faith in the colt by backing him to win £100,000. Come spring it seemed that his owner's judgement was proving sound, for the bay won a sweepstake over a mile at the Newmarket Craven Meeting, in jaunty fashion like his namesake, the 18th-century dandy. He followed this by winning the 2,000 Guineas at 10–1 by half a length from Saccharometer.

Even these two successes failed to sway the backers and Macaroni went to post in the Derby at 10-1. It could not have been a worse day. It poured with rain. But jockey Thomas Chaloner rode the race of his life. From Tattenham Corner it was a two-horse race between Macaroni and the 4–1 favourite Lord Clifden. The latter seemed to be getting the upper hand, leading by a neck until the last few strides. Then Chaloner produced one final effort from his colt to snatch victory by a head. Great was the rejoicing when the news reached Newmarket, probably by carrier pigeon. A peal of bells rang out from All Saints' steeple. Godding was delighted with the result. He was also relieved to be in Epsom. He had an aversion to church bells!

Macaroni went on to win the Drawing Room Stakes at Goodwood and the York and Doncaster Cups, which gave his owner and Newmarket much satisfaction. At stud at Hooton Park he proved a good sire, particularly of brood mares, who produced successful progeny when mated with Bend Or. Macaroni remained at the Park until his death in 1887 at the age of twenty-seven.

2 | Buccaneer and Kisber

IN 1857 LORD DORCHESTER bred *Buccaneer*, by Wild Dayrell out of a mare by Little Red Rover. He was bought by Lord Portsmouth who raced him for four years. From his nineteen starts he won eleven races. He was fast over distances up to a mile, though his trainer found it difficult to train him as he had a splint. He went to stud at a fee of 12 guineas but when his first crop were only yearlings he was sold to Hungary. In him England lost a valuable sire in exchange for 2,600 guineas and a mare called The Gem. He sired *Kisber*, who won the English Derby in 1876, three winners of the German Derby and nine of the Austrian.

The Hungarian Imperial Stud is situated at Kisber and it was here in 1873 that a colt was dropped who was to carry the place name to victory in the Epsom Derby. By Buccaneer out of Mineral by Rataplan, Kisber had an English pedigree. He was a good-looking bay colt, and was sold as a yearling to the Baltazzi brothers for £500. He journeyed to the land of his forebears and went into training. Alexander and Hector Baltazzi were the sons of a Levantine merchant of Turkey, who had the means and the inclination to ensure that they should acquire a sound education. He sent them to Rugby where, besides the acquisition of knowledge and gentlemanly habits, they developed an abiding interest in all forms of sport, especially racing.

The Rothschild family and the Baltazzis were business associates, and shared an enthusiasm for the Sport of Kings. Leopold de Rothschild had inherited the Palace House Stable, Newmarket, from his uncle, Baron Meyer de Rothschild. He allowed the brothers to send a few horses, including Kisber, to be handled by Joseph Hayhoe, an experienced trainer who was responsible for three 1,000 Guineas winners. They included the famous Hannah, winner of the fillies' triple crown in 1871. He also trained Favonius, winner of the 1871 Derby, and Hippia, who won the Oaks in 1867.

Kisber was entered for three races as a two-year-old without any success. It was not until October of the same year that he made his presence felt. He won the seven-furlong Dewhurst Plate at Newmarket. From then on he was marked as a potential Derby winner. He developed well during the winter under Hayhoe's expert eye, but it was disquieting for all concerned that bookmakers were more than willing to take bets. It was rumoured that the colt would never run.

There was some foundation for these rumours. The Baltazzi brothers were in debt to a money-lender for a considerable sum. He was pressing relentlessly for payment. This would have meant the loss of all they possessed, including their string of horses at Palace House Stable. They were at their wit's end when redemption came in the form of Sam Lewis, another money-lender. He paid their debts and advanced them £500. His confidence in Kisber was not misplaced. He started in the Derby at 5–1 and, ridden by Charles Maidment, won by five lengths. Hayhoe was well satisfied and, it is hoped, well rewarded. The Baltazzi brothers were over-joyed with their winnings of £100,000.

Kisber then carried Alexander Baltazzi's colours in France, where he won the Grand Prix de Paris. But returning to Britain to compete in the St Leger he was 'got at' and failed to win. According to John Osborne,

Kisber among the Derby and Oaks winners of 1876, as depicted in *The Illustrated London News*.

J. Sturgess

Palace House Stables, Newmarket, where Kisber was sent for training.

his jockey, known as 'The Bank of England' for his honesty and integrity, Kisber was 'beaten before he even started'. That was the end of his racing career. His early performance at stud was not spectacular. He went to Hungary and then to Gestütt Harzburg in Germany. There he made his mark by siring three German Derby winners, Hardenberg (1893), Sperber (1894) and Trallhetta (1896). This line has not survived.

Flibustier by Buccaneer through Trachenberg and Hannibal continued this branch with *Fels*, a bay colt foaled in 1903 out of Festa by St Simon. He came from the famous Waldfried Stud and was a very good Derby winner in Germany. Of his twenty races he won eighteen and came second in the other two. He sired Laland whose daughter Nereide was one of the best German racemares. She was unbeaten in ten starts and won the German Derby in record time. But the tail male line no longer exists.

3 | Favonius

BARON MEYER AMSCHEL DE ROTHSCHILD (1818–74) was the first Jew to be elected to the Jockey Club. This generous patron of racing was never more popular than in 1871. This was named 'The Baron's Year' for in it he won the Derby, with Favonius, and three other Classics, the 1,000 Guineas, the Oaks and the St Leger with his marvellous filly, Hannah, whom he named after his daughter.

The Baron bred most of his horses himself at Mentmore. Favonius was foaled in 1868, by Parmesan out of Zephyr. He was a rangy chesnut, slow to mature and was not raced as a two-year-old. The following year in his first race, the Newmarket Biennial, he came second to Albert Victor. Nevertheless his owner and trainer were confident that he could succeed in the Derby. He started at 9–1, ridden by the tall Thomas French. This jockey was a great believer in the whip and was prone to punishing his mounts severely. Whether Favonius was hard ridden or not is uncertain, but it is claimed that he won 'comfortably' from Albert Victor and King of the Forest. He did not run in the St Leger, but won the Midsummer Stakes at Newmarket, was second in the Goodwood Cup and won the Brighton Cup.

The following year he was second in the Ascot Gold Cup and won the Goodwood Cup again. His trainer, Joseph Hayhoe, thought so highly of him that he averred, 'I would not take £1,000 for a hair of that horse's tail'. He won only once as a five-year-old, and finished second in the Goodwood Cup. He was then retired to stud at Mentmore. Although he died when he was only nine, he succeeded in siring a Derby winner, *Sir Bevys* (1879).

4 | Cremorne

CREMORNE was foaled in 1869 at the stables of Henry Savile of Rufford Abbey. He was a bay colt by Parmesan out of Rigolboche. His dam had no racing form, having been too unsound to train. Cremorne developed without any physical problems but seemed to have a 'split personality'. On the one hand he had a gargantuan appetite which rendered him so sluggish that he was reputed to fall asleep while on his way to exercise. On the other, he was a horse of merit and when asked to canter or gallop responded immediately and gave of his best. As a two-year-old he won nine of his eleven races and was only beaten in the Prince of Wales' Stakes at York by his gluttony. He had consumed his straw bed which gave him colic.

William Gilbert trained him for the Derby which he won at 3–1 with Charles Maidment up. This jockey rode his best races on horses trained by Gilbert. Henry Savile was delighted with the result. In fact he thought so highly of his trainer that he left instructions in his will for him to choose any five of his horses. When he died in 1880 Gilbert received £12,000 for his quintet at the dispersal sale.

Immediately after his success in the Derby, Cremorne and his owner sailed for France where the colt won the Grand Prix de Paris. This was an unfortunate occurrence to say the least. The British were highly unpopular at the time and the Paris crowd turned very ugly. Mr Savile was advised, for the safety of himself and his victorious colt, to set sail for England with all speed. Accordingly he hastened to Boulogne where he found a gale blowing and the sea very rough. Poor Cremorne had a dreadful crossing, but nothing daunted he proceeded to Ascot to win the Biennial. He followed this by winning two races at York and the Newmarket Derby, though he failed in the Newmarket St Leger.

The following year he did even better by winning the Gold Cup at Ascot by eight lengths and the Alexandra Cup by fifteen lengths. Shortly after these victories he developed a curb which effectively brought his racing career to an end. However, he did appear once more on the racecourse. A bookmaker had offered long odds on his inability to start in the Goodwood Cup, so Cremorne was duly entered and cantered gently round the course at the rear of the field.

Cremorne, from the *Racing Illustrated* of 1896.

Henry Savile's death in 1880 was unfortunate for the horse. Cremorne was sold to a Mr A.S. Lumley. He spent a most sedentary life and was allowed to eat excessively. He lived for just over a year and died suffering from fatty degeneration of the heart. He sired only one foal of any note, a brown filly called Kermesse. Through her fillies she became a taproot mare of great importance.

5 | Sir Bevys

SIR BEVYS WAS FOALED IN 1876 by Favonius out of Lady Langden by Kettledrum. He was bred by Lord Norreys at Wytham, near Oxford. A small brown colt of very modest appearance, he was bought by Baron Lionel de Rothschild, whose extensive property included a stud at Acton. The Baron chose to use the pseudonym of Mr Acton when racing.

Sir Bevys, trained by Joseph Hayhoe, won a race at Newmarket as a two-year-old but was not thought of very highly. However, he trained on to tackle the Derby and was fortunate in his jockey, honest George Fordham, a sympathetic rider, whose style of riding closely resembled that of modern jockeys. Loath to use the whip, he was prone to 'cluck' to his horses and had exceptionally good hands.

Sir Bevys, starting at 20–1, beat the 100–1 outsider Palmbearer by three-quarters of a length, giving Fordham his only Derby win. Not many folk had fancied him, but one gentleman at least had had a good day's racing. Remembering the hero of one of his early poems, Alfred, Lord Tennyson, the Poet Laureate, had placed a bet of £100 to £5. Sir Bevys failed to win the St Leger due to wind trouble and was retired to stud. He made little impression as a sire, so it is to the Woodpecker line that attention must be turned in the search for the Turk's descendants.

PART FIVE

The Woodpecker Line

Derby Winners of The Woodpecker Line

Year	Horse	Jockey	Owner	Colours	Stud
1817	Azor (Ch)	James Robinson	Mr Payne	Pea green	—
1836	Bay Middleton (B)	James Robinson	Lord Jersey	Dark blue, white stripe, black cap	—
1860	Thormanby (Ch)	Henry Custance	Mr J. Merry	Yellow, black cap	—
1837	Phosphorus (B)	George Edwards	Lord Berners	Green and red stripe	—
1846	Pyrrhus the First (Ch)	Samuel Day	Mr J. Gully	Violet, white cap	—
1849	The Flying Dutchman (B)	Charles Marlow	Lord Eglinton	Tartan, buff sleeves & cap	France
1854	Andover (B)	Alfred Day	Mr J. Gully	Violet, white cap	Russia
1856	Ellington (Br)	Thomas Aldcroft	Admiral Harcourt	Fr. grey, crimson hoop, red cap	England
1950	Galcador (Ch)	W. Johnstone	M.M. Boussac	Orange, grey cap	Japan
1969	Blakeney (B)	Ernest Johnson	Mr A. Budgett	Salmon pink, grey sleeves, quartered cap	England

B=Bay   Br=Brown   Ch=Chesnut

Woodpecker

WOODPECKER REPRESENTS the other of the two great branches of King Herod's British line. While Highflyer's progeny were noted for their staying ability, Woodpecker's were renowned for their speed. Highflyer's stock were of every colour, including piebald, whereas those of Woodpecker had the more usual coat colours associated with Thoroughbreds.

Buzzard, a one-eyed chesnut son of Woodpecker, sired three notable colts, *Castrel*, *Rubens* and *Selim* out of an Alexander mare, granddaughter of Eclipse. This mare was such a poor-seeming specimen that the Duke of Queensberry, unable to get £25 for her, gave her to his Newmarket surgeon. Mated with Buzzard, she became a most successful brood mare, producing the three colts mentioned above, a filly named Bronze who won the Oaks, and Quiz.

The important Castrel and Selim branches are dealt with in detail in

Quiz, from a painting by H.B. Chalen, 'Animal Painter to their R.H. the Prince of Wales and Duke and Duchess of York.'

the following chapters. Rubens, a tall heavy colt possessed of a short burst of speed, is remembered primarily for his daughters, who were successful both on the racecourse and at stud.

Quiz was owned by the Reverend Henry Goodricke, whose father Sir Henry Goodricke owned Ribston Hall. The lands of the Hall marched with the manor of Goldsborough, where the Byerley Turk had stood at stud over 100 years before. Quiz's owner, an enthusiastic rider to hounds, was vicar of Aldborough, once a Roman city. Anxious for Quiz to make his mark, he entered him for several races in the south of England. The horse won the Cup at Brocket Hall, the Cup at Reading and at Newmarket, the Jockey Club Plate and several matches. Although he raced until he was eight, his crowning achievement was his success in the 1801 St Leger. A month after that victory, the Reverend Goodricke died aged eighty-two.

PART SIX

The Castrel Branch

The Castrel Branch

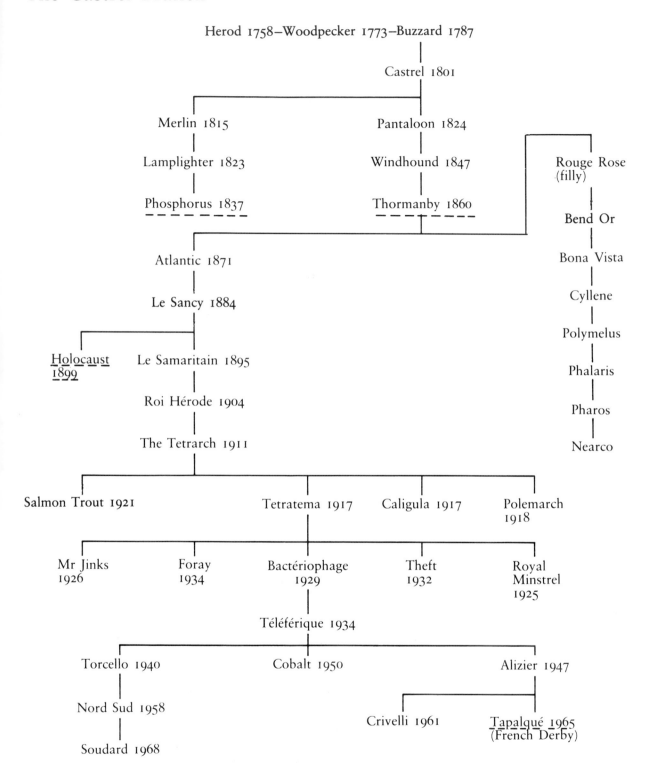

Derby winners and date of win underlined

1 | From Sloane Street to a Rocking Horse

CASTREL, THE ELDEST of the three colts by Buzzard out of a daughter of Alexander, was a handsome 16hh chesnut. Except for being a 'high blower' there was no better horse on the turf at that time. But although of great quality he broke down. He was sent to Parson Harvey's Sloane Street Stables, a last home for many discarded racehorses. Leaving there he stood for some time at The Royells in Cheshire. He finally arrived at Mr Lechmere Charlton's stud near Ludlow. His progeny included *Merlin*, and at the age of twenty-three he sired a colt named *Pantaloon*.

Pantaloon, out of Idalia by Peruvian, was bought by Lord Westminster on the advice of his stud groom, Nutting. He was a huge chesnut marked with black spots. He was hired by the Cawston Stud to cover their newly acquired mare Phryne. It proved a very successful mating. Hemming, the stud groom at Cawston, was told by the mare's owner, Lord John Scott, 'That's the best day's work, Hemming, you ever did in your life, when you hired Pantaloon and bought Phryne.'

Pantaloon was hired the next season for 150 guineas and then 200 guineas, and he never went back. After the first season Phryne had five more foals by him. They were a singular pair. Pantaloon was rather shy with strangers, had an aversion to boys and dogs, and a particular fondness for a certain grey mare. Phryne, who suffered spasms while in foal, was relieved only by the company of a goat. Pantaloon's son Windhound was of no great account, but it is virtually certain that he was the sire of *Thormanby*.

Merlin was the best racehorse of Castrel's progeny. He was bought by Lord Foley for 2,000 guineas. He was unfortunate to break his leg on the racecourse and instead of being put down was subjected to slings and pulleys for some considerable time. This exacerbated his temper and the poor animal grew so wild and unmanageable that only Tyler, his groom, dared approach him, armed with a stout stick. One day another groom ventured into his stall. Merlin particularly disliked this fellow. When eventually the unfortunate man was missed, a search found him savaged and dying with the crazed horse still kneeling on him. Merlin was the sire of Lamplighter, whose bay son *Phosphorus* was owned by Baron Berners and won the Derby in 1837. He had been lame prior to the race and it was amazing that he was able to run at all, let alone win. No doubt he made the day of his somewhat eccentric and quaintly dressed 75-year-old owner. This particular Derby was notable for changes that were introduced to both the method of starting and the day of running. Henceforward the race was started by flag and run on a Wednesday instead of Thursday.

Thormanby, foaled in 1857, was a chestnut colt by Melbourne or Windhound out of Alice Hawthorn, and became the ancestor of two great lines – The Tetrarch and Nearco. Alice, his dam, was an incomparable mare. Foaled at Shipton in 1838, she was by Muley Moloch out of Rebecca, a most intractable character, impossible to train. But Alice herself was in training for seven seasons. She won fifty-two of her seventy-one starts, including the Goodwood Cup, two Doncaster Cups and the Chester Cup. She was said to have 'an action like a hare' and would 'steal along the ground with ears prick'd'. She bred good winners, among them Oulston, the best colt of his year, Lord Fauconberg and Findon. She was eighteen years old when she dropped Thormanby. According to Mat Dawson, who subsequently trained the colt, and 'The Druid', a knowledgeable judge of horseflesh, Alice had looked 'a very hopeless subject'. But by spring she

Alice Hawthorn in 1844, by J.F. Herring.

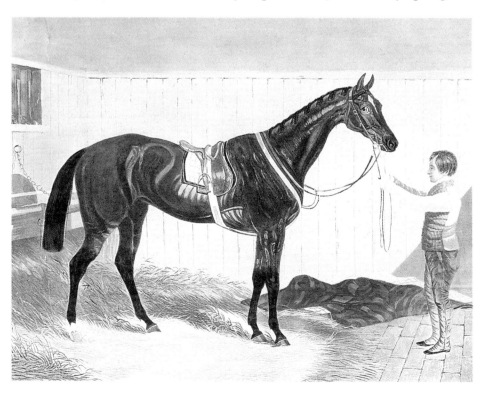

Mat Dawson, trainer of Thormanby.

had gained strength and was sent to be covered by Melbourne. Three weeks later she turned to him and was sent to Windhound. 'Old Alice' is still remembered in the picturesque village of Nun Monkton, near York, where the inn is named after her.

Mr Plummer, his breeder, had difficulty in selling Thormanby as a yearling. Encountering Mat Dawson he persuaded him to go and look at 'one of Alice's which will suit Mr Merry'. So off they set to the Turf Tavern where a bargain was struck. Thormanby changed hands for £350. His new owner, a niggardly, greedy man, did not take to the colt and made Dawson keep him at his own expense until the deal was concluded. It cannnot have been pleasant for him to work for James Merry, a Scottish ironmaster. His boorish manner and obsession with money making were not attractive traits; moreover he suspected all his connections of cheating him. Nevertheless, Dawson set out with a will to train Thormanby. A colt rarely enjoyed a more rigorous regime. He ran no less than fourteen times as a two-year-old, winning ten, including the Biennial Stakes at Royal Ascot, the Gimcrack and the Eglinton Stakes at York.

Although no great beauty Thormanby, with his 'low, lengthy' build and strong, tough legs, was judged by Dawson to be a certainty for the Derby. In the paddock at Epsom he found favour with the critics. When, with his shining coat, he passed the stands he seemed to 'gallop on air'.

Thormanby in 1857, painted by Harry Hall.

He went to the post second favourite at 4–1 with Custance up, and came home a length and a half ahead of Wizard. Mr Merry, merry only when counting his winnings, cleared £85,000. Dawson received £1,000 which, considering his efforts, was hardly handsome. The jockey, on receiving £100, was warned not to let this reward go to his head.

After the Derby Thormanby did little to enhance his reputation until, as a four-year-old, he won the Ascot Gold Cup. Having failed to win the Goodwood Cup, he was retired to stud, where he sired the notable *Rouge Rose* and *Atlantic*.

Rouge Rose was out of Ellen Horne, who was twenty-one when she produced the filly. Rouge Rose's son Bend Or was the sire of Ormonde, one of the greatest horses ever to run on the English turf. The famous Nearco, Nasrullah and Northern Dancer lines stem from him.

Atlantic was a chestnut colt out of Hurricane. Bred by Lord Falmouth, he won the 2,000 Guineas. It is possible that he might have won the Derby had not a slight accident held up his training. As it was he came third to George Fredrick. He sired *Le Sancy*. Foaled in 1884, this powerful grey won twenty-seven of his forty-three starts. As a stallion he was very prolific. He commanded 500 guineas per mare, a high price at the time. Le Samaritain out of Clementina by Doncaster, foaled in 1895, was his son. He won the French St Leger and was the grandsire of Belfonds, who won the French Derby. He is known particularly for his fillies.

Roi Hérode, a grey son of Le Samaritain, was out of the French Oaks winner Roxelane by War Dance and was a stayer with no pretensions to being top class. He was bought by Edward Kennedy of Straffan Stud, Co Kildare, with the idea of rejuvenating the Herod male line. In 1910 he broke down while being prepared for the Chester Cup and was sent forthwith to stand at Mr Kennedy's stud. Most of the good class mares had already been covered, but one, the thirteen-year-old Vahren, a shy breeder, was due to foal late. As a result, it was decided to put her to Roi Hérode. The outcome was the phenomenon popularly known as 'The Rocking Horse'.

2 | The Tetrarch

THE TETRARCH, FOALED ON 22 April 1911, was something of a surprise. He was born a chesnut with black splotches, but as he grew his coat gradually turned grey with white spatters, as if some careless painter had flicked his brush in the colt's direction. Bred at the Straffan Stud, he developed into a tall, ungainly yearling. Mr Kennedy was advised to geld him in the hope that he would make a jumper. However, Atty Persse visited the stud before the Doncaster Sales and liked the look of him.

Persse, who was a master at producing two-year-olds, had trained Nicola, another of Vahren's foals, to be a fine sprinter and thought he could do the same with 'The Rocking Horse'. He saw something in the yearling's gait and mien which others had missed and decided to bid for him. He paid 1,300 guineas which was a good deal in 1912. He would probably have had to pay more if Mr D.M. Gant, who also fancied the colt, had not been dissuaded by his trainer.

Persse passed the colt on to his cousin Dermot McCalmont, a Captain (later Major) in the 7th Hussars. Thus McCalmont became the owner of what was arguably the fastest two-year-old ever seen on a British racecourse. Persse's connection with The Tetrarch did not end there. He undertook the colt's training, which he executed with the same dedication and finesse that he brought to all his endeavours. It was said that when Persse's horses had their first race they never had anything to learn.

In training at Stockbridge The Tetrarch surprised everyone by his rapid progress. He made his racecourse debut on 5 April, winning in a canter at level weights from Captain Symons, who, although aged, went on to win a handicap at Chester the following May also in a canter. Only a week after his first run The Tetrarch took on Captain Symons once more, this time giving him a stone. They were joined by Land of Song, a promising two-year-old who went on to win the Windsor Castle Stakes at Epsom. He was in receipt of 21lb from The Tetrarch, who once again cantered home.

The Tetrarch's potential was not public knowledge and his starting price in the maiden Two-year-old Plate at Newmarket was 5–1. The Tetrarch went to the front of the big field and stayed there, cantering home four lengths ahead of his nearest rival. In his next race, the Woodcote Stakes at Epsom, he beat the favourite Parhelion to the amazement of the latter's jockey, who was confident of victory.

Persse decided to give the colt one more outing before Royal Ascot. He beat two good horses by ten lengths, giving away 35lb weight-for-age. Then at Ascot he won the Coventry Stakes by ten lengths. There was no stopping 'The Spotted Wonder' and he was entered for the National Breeders Produce Stakes at Sandown. It was a misty day and the start was completely obscured from racegoers in the stands. They were expecting to see their favourite romp home 'way ahead of the field'. In fact it was a tremendous feat for him to beat Calandria, in receipt of 17lb, by a neck. What the spectators could not know was that, having collided with the tapes, he was left at the start. Then he hit the quarters of another horse, and his chances at halfway looked very slim. Nevertheless he gamely battled on to win. He raced three times more that season, winning the Rous Memorial Stakes at Goodwood, the Champion Breeders Foal Stakes at Derby and the Champagne Stakes at Doncaster. His seven successes earned his connections £11,336.

Tetratema in 1917.

Although it was intended to run him in the Imperial Produce Stakes he knocked his off-fore fetlock and was unable to start. None the less he was made winter favourite for the Derby. Unfortunately he rapped the same joint again in an exercise gallop. As he tended to plait his forelegs at a slow pace it was feared that he might do himself serious injury. He was therefore taken out of training and dispatched to his owner's stud, a career not at all to his liking. It took all his handler's patience and a good deal of time to persuade him to cover a single mare. He would seize on any excuse to rid himself of this necessity.

He went to stud at a fee of 300 guineas per mare. His first crop of two-year-olds ran in 1918 and their ability placed him ninth in the sires of winners' list. In his first three years at stud he sired fifty foals. In 1919 thirty-four of his forty-two mares were barren, and in 1925 he sired only one foal. In all his ten seasons at stud he was responsible for only 130 foals, but of these eighty were winners.

His son, *The Satrap*, out of Scotch Gift by Symington, was foaled in 1924. Having made a good start by winning the Chesham Stakes at Royal Ascot, the July Stakes and the Chesterfield Stakes at Newmarket and the Richmond Stakes at Goodwood, he split a pastern and could not race again. After an unsuccessful career at stud in America he returned to England, where he produced only one colt of value, the fine stayer *Auralia*. Bred by Mr C.E. Rush and owned by Mrs A. Johnston, Auralia was trained by Reg Day. He was a dark grey horse out of Aura foaled in 1943. He won ten races, in all worth over £12,000. These included the Ascot Gold Vase, the Goodwood Stakes and the Doncaster Cup. He spent his last days in America.

The Tetrarch got three St Leger winners, *Polemarch* (who became a good sire in Argentina), *Caligula* (who went to Germany where he was infertile) and *Salmon Trout*, a disappointing stallion. Before being exported to South Africa Salmon Trout sired Herringbone (winner of the St Leger and the 1,000 Guineas) and *King Salmon*. King Salmon finished second in the Derby. With his four wins, including the Eclipse, he earned £13,731. He was exported to Brazil where he was champion sire in 1943. Another son of The Tetrarch, *Stefan the Great*, sired many winners in the USA.

The Tetrarch imparted his speed above all to Mumtaz Mahal, a brilliant and beautiful animal known as 'The Flying Filly', whose illustrious descendants include Mahmoud and Nasrullah, and to *Tetratema*, a full brother to The Satrap. Tetratema, foaled in 1917, developed into a handsome grey. Bred and owned by Major Dermot McCalmont, he was trained, like his sire, by Atty Persse, who had the satisfaction of seeing the colt finish his two-year-old season unbeaten. Altogether

Diomed, by Francis Sartorius.

The Flying Dutchman (right) with Charles Marlow, watched by his owner Lord Zetland before the start at York. On the left is Voltigeur with Nat Flatman up.

Lexington, by Edward Troye, c. 1865.

Tourbillon and Taxodium (in foreground) at the start of the Grand Prix in 1931.
Painting by André Marchand.

Mumtaz Mahal, one of Marcel Boussac's most successful mares.

he won twelve races, including the 2,000 Guineas, worth £21,776. He stood successfully at stud, being champion sire in 1929 and runner-up three times. His progeny included *Mr Jinks* (winner of the 2,000 Guineas, but only moderate at stud); *Royal Minstrel* (winner of the 2,000 Guineas, and £21,549 in prize money); *First Fiddle* (earned 398,610 dollars); *Theft* (won £10,628, and was a successful sire in Japan); *Foray* (won £9,674 and sired winners in the USA); *Torcello* (sire of *Nord Sud*, winner of the Belgian Derby, Grande Poule des Produits, Grand Prix de Bruxelles, and grandsire of *Soudard*, winner of the Belgian Triple Crown in 1971).

Tetratema's son *Bactériophage*, foaled in 1929 out of Pharmacie by Charles O'Malley, ran only once and was at stud for a mere two years before his death. He was nevertheless an influential stallion, siring *Téléférique*, a chesnut colt out of Beauté de Neige by St-Just. Foaled in 1936, Téléférique became the best two-year-old in France. He was purloined by the Germans and stayed in their country for the duration of the war. Recovered in 1946, he stood in France, where he produced Cobalt (winner of the French 2,000 Guineas in record time, who went to stud in 1954), and Alizier. Téléférique was exported to Brazil in 1951.

Alizier, a bay colt foaled in 1947, was out of the same mare as Cobalt, the Poule d'Essai des Pouliches winner Alazarine by Coronach. Alizier won the Grand Prix at Deauville, the Prix Boiard at St Cloud and the Prix Dangu at Chantilly. He was second in both the Grand Prix de Paris and the Prix de l'Arc de Triomphe. Altogether he won 17½ million francs. He is significant in that the survival of the Castrel branch of the Herod male line in France depends alone on his son *Sigebert*.

In spite of having become infertile, The Tetrarch was retained by his owner. As the years went by his coat gradually turned pure white and his back became dipped. He was a familiar sight making his way down the country lanes to the Post Office with the mail. When he died in August 1935 he was twenty-four and had been sterile for ten years. Major McCalmont buried him in a prominent position at the Ballylinch Stud in Co Kilkenny, where he lies with his son and grandson, Tetratema and Mr Jinks.

Had it not been for his poor fertility and lack of interest in the opposite sex, his considerable contribution to bloodstock breeding would have been greatly enhanced.

PART SEVEN

The Selim Branch

The Selim Branch

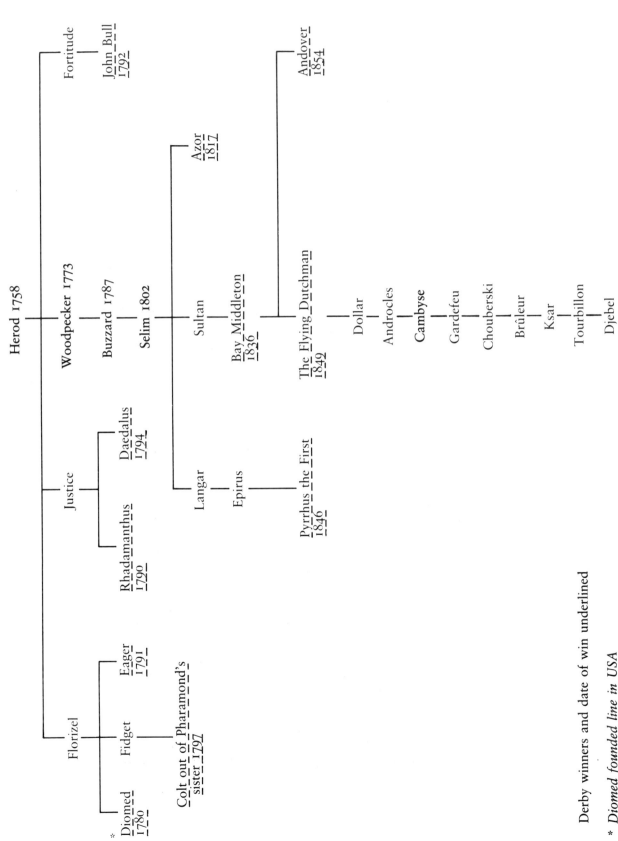

Derby winners and date of win underlined

* Diomed founded line in USA

'He's Bolted with Everyone'

SELIM WAS A HORSE of majestic appearance and temperament. Foaled in 1802 out of a mare by Alexander, he was given to Colonel Leigh by the Prince of Wales, later George IV. He raced successfully over all distances, and became champion sire in 1814. He sired the winners of forty-three races worth £7,711. His progeny included *Sultan*; Azor, a chestnut who won the 1817 Derby at 50–1; and Langar, a fleet Arab-style horse who sired the 1846 Derby winner Pyrrhus the First.

Sultan, out of Bacchante by Williamson's Ditto, was foaled in 1816. He was a quality horse 'whose head might have beseemed a Belvidere Apollo among horses' according to 'The Druid'. His appearance and mien were such that they attracted foreign interest. A story circulating in the clubs at that time related that a Russian nobleman had offered 'two thousand acres and seventy-eight peasants for him'. He was runner-up in the Derby of 1819 and champion sire between 1832 and 1837. Two of his important colts were *Glencoe* and *Bay Middleton*.

Glencoe, foaled in 1831, was a handsome golden chestnut out of Trampoline by Tramp. He belonged to Lord Jersey and won the 2,000 Guineas and the Ascot Gold Cup besides coming third in the Derby. At this time Colonel Jackson of Alabama, USA, instigated a search of British bloodstock for the finest horse that could be bought. He fancied three, of which Glencoe was one, and an offer was made for him. So off to America went this beautiful stallion. He had great influence on American bloodstock through his fillies. Lexington's three most brilliant sons, Asteroid, Kentucky and Norfolk, were all out of Glencoe mares. He lived to the age of twenty-seven.

Bay Middleton was the most important of Sultan's sons. As his name implies he was a bay colt, bred by the Earl of Jersey. He was foaled in 1833 out of Cobweb, the Oaks winner by Phantom. His grandsire Soothsayer had a club foot. This defect skipped a couple of generations and it came out in Bay Middleton in the form of a contracted forefoot. This trait could be seen in lesser forms in many of his descendants.

In *The Post and the Paddock* 'The Druid' writes: 'To see this horse go curling and twisting up to the post, as was his wont, one would have thought him rather weak-built and faint-hearted, whereas he was quite the contrary and only kept from a great Gold Cup by his leg infirmity.' Standing 16.1½hh, he was an impressive looking horse. But he had a wicked expression and was the bane of all with whom he was associated. He did not run at all as a two-year-old.

In February of his Derby year Lord Jersey chanced to encounter James Robinson in London. He begged the jockey to go back with him to see what he could do with the bay. As soon as he arrived he knocked on trainer James Edwards' door. Edwards poked his night-capped head through the window and exclaimed, 'Oh dear! I'm so glad you've come. He's bolted with everyone.'

In the morning his first canter was uneasy. The martingale was too tight and the head lad was summoned. He tried rather warily to loosen it, but the colt managed to tread on it and the martingale broke. With his head free, he took off at a cracking pace, and it was some time before Robinson managed to regain control. He was, however, most impressed with the colt's speed and power. Lord Jersey was so convinced of his worth that he backed him heavily to win the Derby.

Bay Middleton won the Riddlesworth Stakes, the 2,000 Guineas and the Derby, the latter by two lengths at 6–4. Later he won the Buckhurst Stakes at Oxford, the Grandduke Michael Stakes at Newmarket and a match against Muezzin. Then Lord George Bentinck, hoping to win the

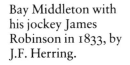

Bay Middleton with his jockey James Robinson in 1833, by J.F. Herring.

Ascot Gold Cup, bought him for £4,000. But the horse finally broke down on his suspect leg and he went to stud at a fee of 30 guineas. Although some of his offspring were unsound or not conducive to training, Bay Middleton became champion sire twice, was second once, third twice and fourth twice. He sired The Flying Dutchman and a bay colt named Andover, winner of the 1854 Derby.

His last days were spent at Danebury where he died at the age of twenty-four. He was buried close to his stable door together with his old companion Crucifix, who survived him by a year. Two cedars were planted in their memory.

Bay Middleton's son *The Flying Dutchman*, foaled in 1846, was a dark bay colt. Lord Eglinton had made an agreement with Colonel Vansittart to buy for 1,000 guineas every perfectly formed foal out of his mare Barbelle by Sandbeck. The Flying Dutchman stood 15.3hh, was roman-nosed, narrow and light through the middle but extremely powerful behind the saddle. Though a very resolute horse, he was ridden occasionally by the daughter of Henry Thompson, Lord Eglinton's stud adviser. She was the finest horsewoman of her day and galloped him with ease.

The colt was trained at Middleham in Yorkshire by Fobert. As a two-year-old he won all his five races, including the July Stakes and the Champagne Stakes at Doncaster. His first outing as a three-year-old was the Derby. With Charles Marlow up he ran a great race to finish half a length in front of Hotspur, with Tadmor third. He was heavily backed by his owner, who made a small fortune, as did the members of the Jockey Club. His trainer was so delighted with the colt's success that he had an ox killed and shared between a hundred poor families of Middleham. His jockey also received a handsome present. He was to die a pauper thirty years later in a Devizes workhouse. In the autumn The Dutchman started a firm favourite for the St Leger, which he won, together with a mile race at Newmarket. It seemed that he was invincible.

The following season he returned to racing fit and well. He started by winning the Ascot Gold Cup on the bridle by eight lengths, with a ten-length win at Goodwood to follow. In 1850 he was entered for the two-and-a-quarter mile Doncaster Cup, his only opponent being Lord Zetland's unbeaten three-year-old Voltigeur. The Dutchman carried 8 stone 12 lb, giving 19 lb to his younger rival. For two days before the race he had been off his food for the first time in his life. Nevertheless, the day before the race Fobert insisted on his galloping over the Cup course.

The management of Lord Eglinton's racing stud always averred that Marlow did not ride to orders. But Richard Johnson, the famous old racing judge, stated in a conversation on the subject in 1897: 'The cause of the horse being beaten was that Lord Eglinton said to Marlow, after

The Flying Dutchman beating Voltigeur at York, 1851, by J.F. Herring.

he was up, "Now go and make an example of him". I was quite close to him when the order was given.'

Though a fairly steady jockey as a rule, Marlow had been drinking. He set off at a spanking gallop and in the final furlong The Dutchman faltered. Seizing his opportunity, Flatman drove Voltigeur on strongly to win the race. The silent crowd, most of whom had backed the local hero at 4–1, were nonplussed. Lord Eglinton was white and shaken and the jockey in a flood of alcoholic tears.

Previous to the race at Doncaster, The Dutchman had been sold to Henry Stafford-Thompson on behalf of the Stud Company at Rawcliffe. He was to change hands after the race, which everyone connected with the newly-formed stable expected him to win. Imagine their consternation when he failed. Their whole venture would be of little worth without the prestige of a winning stallion. Mr Thompson persuaded Lord Eglinton to keep the horse in training for a return match. In the spring of 1851 the contest between the two great horses took place on the Knavesmire in York. Yorkshire folk, young and old, on horseback and on foot, came in their thousands to watch the race. There had not been such a gathering since Eugene Aran was hanged there for murder in the previous century. Most of the crowd favoured Voltigeur, whose owner Lord Zetland was a Yorkshire peer. The big wagers were placed on The Flying Dutchman.

This time Voltigeur set the pace, with his opponent in close touch. The Dutchman made his challenge in the final furlong and beat Voltigeur by a length. He never ran again. At stud he covered fifty mares in his first season, which was asking too much of him. He was not considered to be a successful sire in England. He was an unprepossessing horse, standing 15.2½hh, with a long back which his progeny inherited and which did not equip them for flat racing. However, he proved through Le Batare, Benazet, The Brick, Woodbury Hill, Tom Sawyer and others to be one of the best steeplechase sires of the day. His son Ellington out of Ellerdale was his only success on the Flat, winning the Derby in 1856. He was a lengthy brown horse with a coarse head and big feet, which helped him to plough through the sticky ground and come home at 20–1. He had no success as a sire.

As steeplechase horses were considered of no great importance in England, The Dutchman was exported to France for £4,000. There he established a most important branch of the Herod line. Through his son *Dollar* the dynasty can be traced to the present day.

PART EIGHT

The French Connection

The French Connection

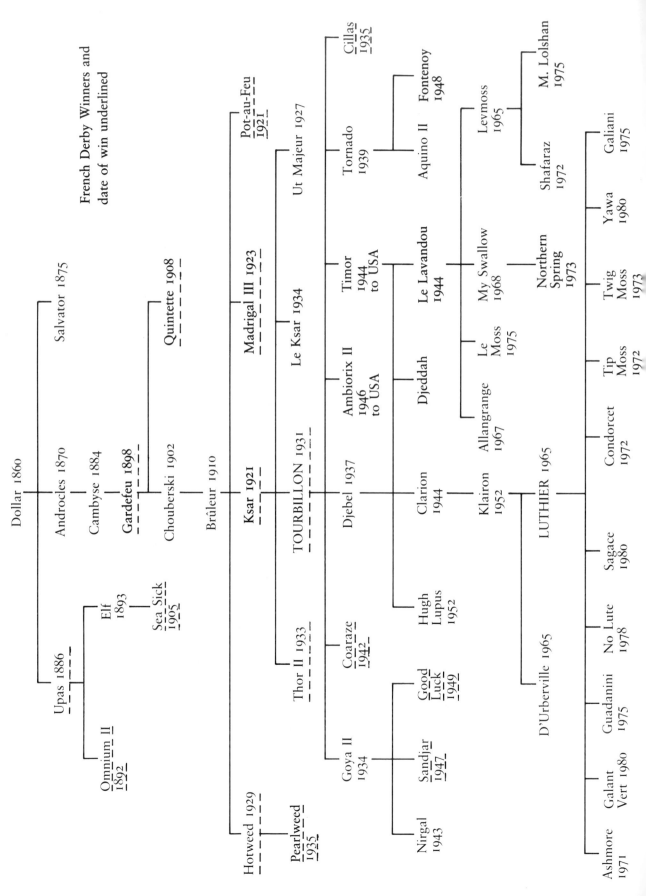

French Derby Winners and
date of win underlined

I | 'Très Puissant'

With the export of The Flying Dutchman, the Selim branch of the Herod line continued in France until Hethersett was foaled in 1959. The Dutchman's son *Dollar* was bred by Auguste Lupin. He was a medium-sized bay or brown colt out of Payment by Shane, foaled in 1860. Blessed with a perfect temperament, he grew to be *très puissant* but easy to train.

As a two-year-old he had no success, but a year later he won three of his seven starts. He was sent over from France to join Hayhoe's Newmarket Stable. This uncompromising trainer adhered to the tradition of making a colt pay for his keep. Dollar had plenty of work. During his stay he won the Northamptonshire Stakes, an important race of the day. Over in France he won the Prix de l'Impératrice, returning to England to win the Goodwood Cup and the Brighton Cup in quick succession. Retired to stud in France, he proved to be a fertile sire of great influence. He died at the age of twenty-seven. Of his progeny, three colts came to prominence: *Salvator*, *Upas* and *Androcles*.

Salvator was a chesnut out of Sauvagine by Ion, foaled in 1872. He was a big, attractive individual of good appearance and great power. He was never beaten and succeeded in winning the French Derby and the Grand Prix de Paris at Longchamp. *Upas* was foaled in 1883 out of Rose Mary by Skirmisher. He was successful in the French Derby as a three-year-old, and at four won the Prix du Cadran over two and a half miles at Longchamp and the Prix Dangu over the same distance at Chantilly. His son Omnium II, a chesnut foaled in 1892 out of Bluette by Wellingtonia, also won the French Derby, despite being built like a camel, with large spread feet, a characteristic which he passed on to Ksar through his dam and his sire's dam.

Androcles, a bay or brown colt foaled in 1870 out of Alabama by Light or Serious, is notable in that he carried on the line to *Cambyse*. This colt never won a Classic but he did gain nine victories and five places out of fourteen starts as a three-year-old. At four he won the Goodwood Cup. He was a bay foaled in 1884 out of Cambuse by Plutus.

Gardefeu, by Cambyse out of Bougie by Bruce, was a bay colt foaled in 1895. He won the French Derby and was in his day judged second only to Le Roi Soleil. He was a sire of some importance noted especially for producing exceptional brood mares. Two of his sons, *Quintette* and *Chouberski*, have some claim to fame. Quintette won the French Derby in 1909 in a dead heat with Sea Sick, and *Chouberski* carried on the Herod Line.

Chouberski, a bay colt foaled in 1902, was out of Campanule by The Bard. His only victory was disputed and after breaking a pastern he was retired to stud. He left a considerable imprint on Thoroughbred breeding mainly through La Bidouze, dam of Biribi, who became a sire of some importance, and Brûleur. Born in 1910, out of Basse-Terre, daughter of Omnium II, the bay Brûleur was the best colt ever owned by M. E. de St Alary, a racing figure well known and respected on both sides of the Channel. Brûleur was a top class horse, compact and strong, with an imposing presence. He won the 1913 Grand Prix de Paris and the French St Leger. Retired to stud, he got stock who were reputed to be highly strung, but he produced no less than four French Derby winners: *Madrigal III*, *Hotweed*, *Pot-au-Feu* and *Ksar*.

Madrigal III, a bay colt out of La Maddaloun, won the 1926 French

'M. Lupin's Dollar, winner of The Goodwood Cup', from *The Illustrated London News*, 1864.

Derby in front of Biribi, Nino and Asterus. He was exported to stud in Argentina in 1935 but left little mark. *Hotweed*, who won the Grand Prix de Paris as well as the 1929 French Derby, was a bay colt out of Seaweed by Spearmint. He was exported to England, where his only foal of note was the French Derby winner Pearlweed out of Pearl Maiden. He was destroyed in 1940 at the early age of fourteen.

Pot-au-Feu was a chestnut foaled in 1921 out of Polly Peachum by Spearmint. He stood for one year in England, two in France and was then exported to America. He failed to produce good stock in all three countries.

Other worthy progeny of Brûleur included *Brûlette* and *Palais Royal II*. The last named was a tough chestnut horse foaled in 1925 out of Puntarenas by Maintenon. He won six races in France, the Grand International at Ostend and the 1928 Cambridgeshire in England. Brood mares were the best of his progeny.

Brûlette, a light bay full sister to Hotweed, won once as a two-year-old and had two easy successes as a three-year-old, when her owner Colonel Birkin refused £10,000 for her. She won the 1931 Oaks in England in style and later the Prix du Cadran, France's Gold Cup, but as a brood mare she failed to produce any outstanding foals except Tropical Sun, who finished third in the Oaks and was the granddam of Vaguely Noble.

Priori a bay colt foaled in 1922 out of Primavista by St Bris, won the Prix de l'Arc de Triomphe.

Ksar, a chestnut colt, was foaled in 1918 out of Kizil Kourgan, whose sire was the 1895 French Derby winner Omnium II. Kizil Kourgan was one of the best racing fillies ever to run in France. She was nineteen years old when she produced Ksar, having failed to breed anything outstanding up to that point. Ksar won the French Derby and the Prix de l'Arc de Triomphe and spent some thirteen years at stud in France, before going to the United States, where he died three years later. Undoubtedly his greatest contribution to modern bloodstock was his son *Tourbillon*.

At stud Ksar soon proved to be a sire of great ability. In England *Ut Majeur* and *Le Ksar* were two of his successful sons. *Ut Majeur*, a bay foaled in 1927 out of a mare named Uganda by Bridaine, won the Cesarewitch, and was sent to Hungary in 1936 after three or four seasons at stud in England. *Le Ksar* was bred in France by Leon Volterra. He was a bay colt out of Queen Iseult by Teddy. M. E. de St Alary bought him as a yearling for £3,000 in a private transaction. His most important victory was in the 1937 2,000 Guineas. During the war years he stood at stud in England and was then exported to Argentina.

Thor II, a bay colt out of Lasarte by Alcantara II, won the French Derby for Marcel Boussac in 1933, ridden by Charlie Elliot. He followed this by winning the French Gold Cup and was second in the Ascot Gold Cup where he beat Hyperion.

Tourbillon, the 'whirlwind', was foaled in 1928 and had a faultless pedigree. He was out of a mare called Durban, who was by Durbar II, the 1914 Derby winner out of the French 1,000 Guineas winner Banshee by Irish Lad, and belonged to Marcel Boussac's stud. Tourbillon won the French Derby ridden, like Thor II and Djebel, by Charlie Elliot whose instinct and good judgement were responsible in some measure for Marcel Boussac's many victories.

It is not as a racehorse, however, but as an outstanding stallion that Tourbillon has gained his reputation. He went to stud in 1932 and was four times champion sire in France. He died in 1954 at the age of twenty-six. At that time his progeny, who mostly preferred firm going, had won some 390 races valued at 102,176,500 francs in France and forty-two races in England worth £45,529. In addition to those mentioned, his progeny stood in many countries, including Argentina, South Africa, the USA, Australia and New Zealand.

2 | Sons of Tourbillon

GOYA II WAS THE ELDEST of Tourbillon's notable colts. Foaled in 1934 out of Zariba by Sardanapale, he was a bright bay who distinguished himself between the ages of two and six in France, England and and Germany. His dam was one of Marcel Boussac's most highly regarded mares.

Not outstanding in appearance, he proved himself a winner on the racecourse. He sailed home in the Gimcrack Stakes and the St James's Palace Stakes and came second in the Middle Park Stakes, the Champion Stakes and the English 2,000 Guineas behind Le Ksar. At stud he produced two French Derby winners, *Sandjar* foaled in 1944 out of Zulaikaa, who went to stud in Brazil in 1952, and *Good Luck*, foaled in 1946 out of Ma Canaille by The MacNab, who came home in front of Ambiorix and Violoncelle. He was exported to Brazil in the same year.

Now and again a colt of great beauty and presence is produced who also excels on the racecourse. Such a one was Tourbillon's bay son *Caracalla II*, who ran in the colours of Marcel Boussac. He was born in 1942 out of a famous mare named Astronomie by Asterus. She was also the dam of Arbar by Djebel. Caracalla was never beaten, counting among his victories the Grand Prix de Paris, the French St Leger and the Prix de l'Arc de Triomphe. After such a successful career his connections hoped for great things from him at stud. They were bitterly disappointed when their handsome stallion proved worthless as a sire.

Mention must also be made of *Goyama*, foaled in 1943 out of a speedy mare named Devineress. He won eight races in France besides the Grand Prix de St Cloud. In England he won the Ormonde Stakes at Chester and the Coronation Cup at Epsom. Goya also sired Sakountala (the dam of Hugh Lupus), Corteira who won the French 1,000 Guineas, and *Nirgal*. This colt was bred in France by Marcel Boussac. Out of Castillane by Cameronian, he was a bay, foaled in 1943. Trained by C.H. Semblat, in his first season he won the Prix Robert Papin, the Prix Morny and the Grand Critérium. Later he divided his time between England and France where he won fourteen races. He became a leading sire of juveniles when exported to America in 1948. He died at the age of sixteen.

Tornado, as his name implies, was fast though not as furious as his son

Tourbillon's Sons

Colt	Year	Dam	Achievements	Stud
Goya II (B)	1934	Zariba	Gimcrack Stakes, 2nd Middle Park Stakes	Champion in France
			St James's Palace Stakes, 2nd in English 2,000 Guineas and The Champion Stakes	USA
Cillas (B)	1935	Orlanda	French Derby	Ireland
Djebel (B)	1937	Loika	French Derby and English and French 2,000 Guineas Prix de l'Arc de Triomphe etc.	Champion in France
Tornado (B/B)	1939	Roseola	2nd in French Derby and St Leger	France
Coaraze (B)	1942	Corrida	2nd in Grand Prix de St Cloud	To Brazil in 1954
Caracalla II (B)	1942	Astronomie	Ascot Gold Cup Grand Prix de Paris	France
Tourment (B)	1942	Fragment	2,000 Guineas St Leger	France
Turmoil (B)	1945	Blue Iras	French Gold Cup, Grand Prix, Deauville	France Ireland
Ambiorix II (B)	1946	Lavendula	2nd in French Derby	USA
Cagire II (B)	1947	Source Sucrée	Won £13,204, King George VI Stakes, Ormonde Stakes	Ireland
Timor (Ch)	1944	Samya	Stakes winner in France incl. Prix Hocquart	Argentina

Aquino II. Foaled in 1939, Tornado was a dark bay out of a mare named Roseolo by Swynford. As a three-year-old he won the Prix Daru and Prix Lupin at Longchamp. He was second by a nose to Magister in the French Derby and third in the Grand Prix de Paris by a head to Tifinar. He was narrowly beaten by Djebel in the Prix de l'Arc de Triomphe. At four he was victorious in the Ganay-ex-Sablons at Longchamp. His daughter Tahiti won the French Oaks. Of his sons, *Aquino II* and *Fontenoy* have some claim to fame.

Aquino II was bred by the Marquis de Nicolay. He was a bay colt out of Apulia by Apelle. He won twice as a two-year-old and took the fancy of the Maharanee of Baroda, who paid a small fortune for him. He stayed in France but did not come up to expectations, winning only the Prix Daru. He then joined the Newmarket stables of Fred Armstrong, who sent him out to win the Ascot Gold Cup. He was bad tempered, unpredictable and hardly a pleasure to deal with. He started in the Goodwood Cup, pranced about, refused to race and finally ducked out, then redeemed himself somewhat by winning the Doncaster Cup. He finished his chequered career at stud in Poland.

Tornado's bay son *Fontenoy* was the sire of *Tropique*. Foaled in 1952, the latter was a handsome bay colt out of Aurore Boreale by Massine. He was owned by Baron Guy de Rothschild and trained by G. Watson in France. His two-year-old career was marred by a split pastern, but the following year he won three times, the Prix de Boulogne at Longchamp, the Prix le Marois at Le Tremblay and the Prix de la Côte Normande at Deauville. At four he was a first class middle-distance horse. He counted among his successes the mile-and-a-half Coronation Cup at Epsom and the ten-furlong Eclipse Stakes at Sandown. He sired *Paveh*, winner of the Irish 2,000 Guineas, and *Creole*, who carried Lord Rosebery's colours to victory in the Stewards' Cup.

Djebel in 1952.

Djebel's Sons

Colt	Year	Dam	Achievements	Stud
Clarion (B)	1944	Columba	Best 2 yr. old Grand Critérium	France
Arbar (B)	1944	Astronomie	King George VI Stakes, Ascot Gold Cup, Prix du Cadran – 2nd St Leger – Goodwood Cup	France
Le Lavandou (B)	1944	Lavande	Portland Handicap	Ireland
Djeddah (Ch)	1945	Djezima	6 races in France, Eclipse and Champion Stakes	USA
My Babu (B)	1945	Perfume	Won £29,830 incl. 2,000 Guineas 5 wins at two years, 23 wins at three, 3 at four	England & USA
Galcador (Ch)	1947	Pharyva	St Firmin, Daphnis, English Derby	Japan
Argur (Ch)	1949	Bouillabaisse	Queen Anne Stakes	Argentina
Hugh Lupus (B)	1952	Sakountala	Champion Stakes, Irish £2,000	Ireland
Entente Cordiale (B)	1951	Herringbone	12 races incl. Doncaster Cup	England

3 | Djebel

IT WAS A LUCKY DAY for Boussac when his in-foal mare
Löika, by Gay Crusader, was offered at the December sales and failed
to attract a buyer. For the foal which she dropped in 1937 turned out
to be one of the best of the Byerley line. Named Djebel, he grew to be a
smallish, hardy bay of real quality. He was trained at Chantilly by M.A.
Swann, who ran him four times as a two-year-old. He won a five-furlong
race at Longchamp and was second on three occasions, including the Prix
Morny at Deauville. He was then sent to Newmarket, where he won the
Middle Park Stakes. The following season he won both the English and
French 2,000 Guineas, plus the Prix de l'Arc de Triomphe. The intention
had been to run in the English Derby, but by that time the Second World
War had broken out and France had been overrun. It was impossible to
ship him to England where he would, arguably, have beaten the eventual
winner, Pont L'Evêque.

Fearing that the horse might find his way to Germany, as so much
bloodstock did, Marcel Boussac wisely spirited him away to the South
of France where it was hoped he would be safe. There he stayed until
things settled down somewhat and a curtailed racing programme was
resumed. In the middle of October he started to race again. He entered
the very late running of the combined 1,000 and 2,000 Guineas and beat
all comers. He was kept in training as a five-year-old, when he was considered even better than in his younger days. Altogether he won fifteen
races, and from twenty-two starts he was never out of the first three. His
winnings in France amounted to 4,153,760 francs and in England £6,115.
Added to this was about 200,000 francs in place money.

This valuable stallion retired to stud in 1943. He immediately made his
mark and was four times champion sire in France. Some of his most successful colts are listed below and discussed in more detail on the following
pages. But it must not be forgotten that he was an equally potent sire of
fillies. These included Djerba, one of his first crop (Cheveley Park Stakes),
Djelfa (French 1,000 Guineas), Montenica (French Oaks), Djebellica (Irish
Oaks), Apollonia (French 1,000 Guineas and Oaks), and Janiari (Newmarket Oaks and Prix Vermeille).

Arbar, described as 'petit et très courageux', was a good stayer with

Marcel Boussac and
(below) the Boussac
stud farm at Fresnay.

a fine turn of finishing speed. He was bred in France by Marcel Boussac. Foaled in 1944, he was a bay colt out of the same dam as Caracalla II, Astronomie by Asterus. He was trained by C.H. Semblat, who had ridden his first winner at the age of thirteen and later partnered many of Boussac's horses with great success. After a particularly severe fall he retired from riding and took up training for the same stable. Under Semblat's guidance, Boussac's orange jacket and grey cap led the way home in a great number of races both in Britain and in France over a period of fifteen years.

Arbar showed his ancestry in his Arab-like head, which he carried proudly to victory in the King George VI Stakes, the Ascot Gold Cup and the Prix du Cadran. At stud he sired Altana (second in the English Oaks in 1954) and Arcor (second in the Derby of 1962). His son Abdos won the Grand Critérium and was an excellent sire of brood mares.

Le Lavandou was a bay colt foaled in 1944. His dam Lavande by Rustom Pasha had won three races in France. He was a speedy two-year-old and won the Portland Stakes at Doncaster. At stud in Ireland he was doing very well and great things were expected of him, but he died young.

He left behind *Le Levanstell*, who was to prove a very successful stallion. Bred by the McGrath Stud Company of Ireland, he was owned by Joseph McGrath and trained by Seamus McGrath. He was foaled in 1957 out of Stella's Sister and was a good-looking bay who started his racing career very well. He won three of his four starts as a two-year-old, including the six-furlong Railway Stakes at the Curragh and the six-furlong Birdcatchers' Stakes at Naas, and finished second in the National Produce Stakes at the Curragh. Much to his trainer's dismay, he ran seven times as a three-year-old without success, though he did manage to finish second in the Jersey Stakes. At four he regained his form and was successful in the seven-furlong Woodbine Stakes at Leopardstown and two races over a mile – the Sussex Stakes at Goodwood and the Queen Elizabeth II Stakes at Ascot. He was unsuccessful the following year and retired to stud having earned £11,361. At stud he was particularly noted for siring good stayers. His filly Sweet Mimosa won the French Oaks in 1970 and two of his sons, *Levmoss* and *My Swallow*, also made their mark.

Levmoss, a bay colt out of Freemoss, daughter of Ballymoss, was foaled in 1965. Like his sire, Le Levanstell, he was trained by Seamus McGrath. As a two-year-old he ran only twice, winning the six-furlong Clashwilliam Plate at Gowran Park. At three he divided his time between England and Ireland. He won the ten-furlong Finglas Stakes at Phoenix Park, the Oxfordshire Stakes at Newbury over a mile and five furlongs and the two-mile Leopardstown November Handicap carrying 9st 4lb. He came fourth in the Lingfield Derby Trial and the Queen's Vase at Royal Ascot and third in the French St Leger.

Levmoss and W.W.
Williamson after
winning the Ascot Gold
Cup in 1969.

His connections were well satisfied and acknowledged that he was a
stayer of quality but hardly a highflyer. However, in 1969 his career really
took off and he proved himself the champion of Europe over distances
from a mile and a half to two miles and a half. In April he ran a close
third in the two-mile Prix Jean Prat at Longchamp. In May on the same
course he won the Prix du Cadran over two and a half miles, beating
his old rivals Zamazaan and Samos III by a head and neck. In June he
was favourite for the Ascot Gold Cup, run over the same distance. He
beat Torpid by four lengths. In September after a short rest he won the
mile and three-quarter Leinster Handicap at the Curragh by three lengths
carrying 10st 10lb.

He was hardly expected to win the 1969 Prix de l'Arc de Triomphe at
Longchamp. Although he stayed for ever it was feared that he lacked the
necessary finishing speed. Some good horses were matched against him
including the King George VI and Queen Elizabeth Stakes winner Park
Top, Grandier, the Derby hero Blakeney, Prince Regent and Crepellana,
winner of the French Oaks. In the event, ridden by Bill Williamson, he set
off with his usual determination and won by a length and a half from Park
Top, with Grandier three lengths back in third. He earned over £88,000

My Swallow and Lester Piggott winning the Woodcote Stakes at Epsom on Derby Day, 1970.

that day. He then retired to stud in Ireland at a fee of 3,000 guineas. His progeny featured prominently in the sales.

Le Levanstell's other important male heir, *My Swallow*, was bred in Ireland by Mr A. Walsh. He was foaled in 1968, the second foal of Darrigle by Vilmoray. He developed into a strong and beautiful bay standing 16.3hh. At the Dublin Sales he was bought by Lord Harrington for David Robinson for 5,000 guineas. Trained by Paul Davey, he matured early, looked impressive and started his two-year-old career at York in May where he won the five-furlong Zetland Stakes by three lengths. In June he attempted an extra furlong in the Woodcote Stakes at Epsom, and was again successful. Off he went to France in June where he won the five-furlong Prix du Bois at Longchamp. A month later, after a real battle with Mill Reef, he won the five-and-a-half-furlong Prix Robert Papin at Maisons-Laffitte, and in August he was successful in the six-furlong Prix Morny at Deauville. He followed these victories with another in the seven-furlong Prix de la Salamandre at Longchamp in September, and in October took the Grand Critérium, the most prestigious race for two-year-olds. As a result he was placed top of both English and French Free Handicaps, being the first horse to win the three important French two-year-old races, the Prix Robert Papin, the Prix Morny and the Grand Critérium since *Nirgal* in 1945. His French winnings alone amounted to £85,465.

Poor My Swallow; is it any wonder that he failed to come up to scratch as a three-year-old? He had been shipped to and fro and engaged in such a heavy programme. Perhaps with a more sympathetic owner he might have fulfilled his potential. As it was, he did manage to finish third in the 2,000 Guineas, beaten only by that superlative pair Brigadier Gerard and Mill Reef. He was seen and fancied during the 1971 season by Irving Allen and was bought for £400,000 to stand at the Derisley Wood Stud at Newmarket. In his first two crops he sired thirty individual winners of forty-three races worth over £100,000. These included: *Northern Spring* (Gran Criterium Premia Primi Passi [Gr.3], Champion two-year-old of Italy, 1975); *Outer Circle* (Champion two-year-old Trophy, Princess Margaret Stakes, Kingsclere Stakes, fourth in the Cheveley Park Stakes [Gr.1]), *All Hope* (Ribero Stakes, third in the Dewhurst Stakes, Blue Riband Stakes); *Command Freddie* (Prix la Rochette [Gr.3]), and *Sporty Girl* (Belgian Oaks).

Netherkelly, a brown colt by Le Levanstell out of Princess Quay by Babur by My Babu, was foaled in 1970. He raced on the flat over distances from five furlongs to a mile and six furlongs and also went jumping, winning a total of eight races under both Rules. He also finished second in the Coventry Stakes at Royal Ascot (Gr.2), and third in the Prix Hérode at Longchamp. He was retired to stud at Denton, Northamptonshire, and was a featured stallion in 1987.

Clarion, one of Djebel's first foals, was born in 1944, a bay colt out of Columba by Colorado. In France he became the best two-year-old of his generation. He won the Grand Critérium at Longchamp and later was second in the Lincolnshire Handicap. Together with *Hugh Lupus* and *Le Lavandou* he assured the continuation of the Herod line in England.

Clarion's son *Klairon* was a bay colt out of Kalmia by Kantar. Foaled in 1952 he became the best two-year-old of his generation, winning six races, including the French 2,000 Guineas. In the 2,000 Guineas at Newmarket he finished third, beaten only a neck and a short head by Our Babu and Tamerlane. When retired to stud he stood first at the King Edward Place Stud near Swindon, then moved to the Kingswood Stud, and finally went to the Barton Stud near Newmarket. Frank Berry, stud groom at Kingswood, described him as 'a medium sized, rich brown, high quality horse with a lovely temperament'.

Though not very enthusiastic about covering mares, he was fertile and sired winners of over £650,000, including Monade, winner of the Oaks and Prix Vermeille, Altissima (French 1,000 Guineas), D'Urberville

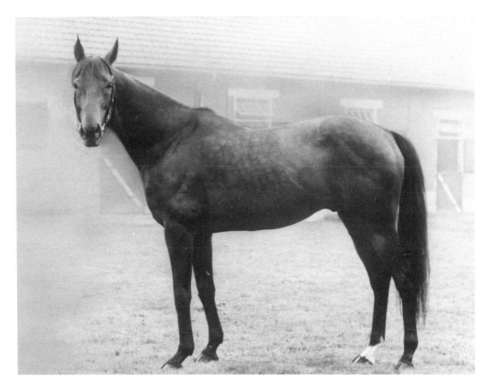

Klairon, 'the best two-year-old of his generation.'

(leading sprinter), *Luthier* and *Lorenzaccio*. His versatility is shown by his progeny, which range from sprinters to stayers. One season a mare named Phoenissa by The Phoenix was sent to Klairon by the Airlie Stud. She was later examined and the vet was of the opinion that she was empty. But before washing her out and starting again it was decided to wait a few days. After the weekend a tiny embryo was discovered. How near was the loss of that beautiful fiery colt who raced under the name of *Lorenzaccio* and won a total of £87,936.

Luthier and his sons carry the connection in France into the present day. He was foaled in 1965, out of Flute Enchantée by Cranach, and was a bay horse of striking appearance whose four wins earned 953,285 francs. He raced over distances of between seven and eleven furlongs, and his successes included The Prix Jacques Le Marois at Deauville (Gr.1); three wins at Longchamp, The Prix Lupin (Gr.1), the Prix Noailles (Gr.2) and the Prix Ganay, (Gr.1), and fourth place in the Grand Critérium, (Gr.1). He went to stud in 1970 and was the sire of winners of over 650 races worth more than 55 million francs. He was four times champion stallion in France before his death in 1981, and was subsequently leading sire of brood mares in 1986.

Principal Progeny of Luthier

Sagace (Fr.)

Won Prix de l'Arc de Triomphe (Gr.1), Longchamp.
Prix d'Isaphan (Gr.1), Longchamp.
Prix Ganay (Gr.1), Longchamp.
Prix du Conseil de Paris (Gr.2).
Prix Niel (Gr.3), Longchamp.
Prix Foy (twice), (Gr.3), Longchamp.
2nd Prix de l'Arc de Triomphe (Gr.1), Longchamp.
Prix Ganay (Gr.1), Longchamp.
Sire in USA.

Riverton

Classic sire in New Zealand.

St Cyrien (Fr.)

Champion two-year-old and Horse of the Year in France.
Won Grand Critérium (Gr.1), Longchamp.
Prix Saint Roman (Gr.3), Longchamp.
2nd Prix de Fontainebleau (Gr.3), Longchamp.
Sire in France.

Guadanini (Fr.)

Won Grand Prix de Saint Cloud (Gr.1), Saint Cloud.
Prix Jean de Chaudenay (Gr.2), Saint Cloud.
Grand Prix de Vichy (Gr.3), Vichy.
La Coupe (Gr.3), Longchamp.
Caballero Handicap. Hollywood Park.
2nd Prix Hocquart (Gr.2), Longchamp.
4th Prix Foy (Gr.3), Longchamp.
Sire in France.

No Lute

Won Prix Lupin (Gr.1), Longchamp.
Sire in France.

King Luthier

Won Prix Kergorlay (Gr.2), Deauville.
Warren Stakes (L.), Epsom.
2nd Grand Prix d'Evry (Gr.2), Evry.
4th Geoffrey Freer Stakes (Gr.2), Newbury.

Bois de Grace (Fr.)

Won Prix Greffulhe (Gr.2), Longchamp.
2nd Sierra Nevada Handicap (Gr.3), Santa Anita.
3rd Prix du Jockey Club, (Gr.1), Chantilly.
      Prix de Conde (Gr.3), Longchamp.
      Exceller Stakes, Hollywood Park.
Sire in Japan.

Montcontour (Fr.)

Won Prix Hocquart (Gr.2), Longchamp.
      Hardwicke Stakes (Gr.2), Royal Ascot.
2nd Prix de Courcelles (L.), Longchamp.
3rd King George VI and Queen Elizabeth Stakes (Gr.1), Ascot.
4th Grosser Preis von Baden (Gr.1), Baden-Baden.
Sire abroad.

Luthier.

Tip Moss (Fr.)

Won Grand Prix d'Evry (Gr.2), Evry.
    Grand Prix de la Ville de Toulouse (L.), Toulouse.
2nd Grosser Preis von Baden (Gr.1), Baden-Baden.
    Preis von Europa (Gr.1), Köln.
    Prix Daphnis (Gr.3), Evry.
    Grand Prix Prince Rose (L.), Ostend.
3rd Grand Prix de Saint-Cloud (Gr.1), Saint-Cloud.
    Prix Dollar (Gr.2), Longchamp.
    Prix du Conseil de Paris (Gr.2), Longchamp (twice).
    Prix Foy (Gr.3), Longchamp.
    Grand Prix de Nantes (L.), Nantes.
4th Prix Ganay (Gr.1), Longchamp.
Sire in France.

Ashmore (Fr.)

Won Grand Prix de Deauville (Gr.2), Deauville (twice).
    Prix Jean de Chaudenay (Gr.2), Saint-Cloud.
    Prix de Menneval (L.), Deauville.
    Prix de Reux (L.), Deauville.
2nd Coronation Cup (Gr.1), Epsom.
    Grand Prix de Saint-Cloud (Gr.1), Saint-Cloud (twice).
3rd Prix Royal Oak (Gr.1), Longchamp.
    Prix Maurice de Nieuil (Gr.2), Saint-Cloud.
Sire in UK and Germany.

Condorcet (Fr.)

Won Prix Maurice de Nieuil (Gr.2), Saint-Cloud.
    Prix Omnium II (L.), Saint-Cloud.
2nd Poule d'Essai des Poulains (Gr.1), Longchamp.
    Prix Exbury (Gr.3), Saint-Cloud.
    Grand Prix de Nantes (L.), Nantes.
3rd Prix Jean de Chaudenay (Gr.3), Saint-Cloud.
    Prix Thomas Bryon (Gr.3), Saint-Cloud.
    Prix de la Côte Normande (Gr.3), Deauville.
    La Coupe de Maisons-Laffitte (Gr.3), Maisons Laffitte.
    Prix de Foals (L.), Deauville.
    Grand Prix de Nantes (L.), Nantes.
Sire in UK and S. Africa.

Twig Moss (Fr.)

Won Prix Noailles (Gr.2), Longchamp.

2nd Prix du Jockey Club (Gr.1), Chantilly.
Prix de Courcelles (L.), Longchamp.
3rd Prix Hocquart (Gr.2), Longchamp.
2nd Leading Sire in Australia 1985–86.

Yawa

Won Grand Prix de Paris (Gr.1), Longchamp.
Premio Roma (Gr.1), Rome.
Blathwayt Stakes, Bath.
2nd Prix Jean Prat (Gr.2), Longchamp (twice).
Prix Vicomtesse Vigier (Gr.2), Longchamp.
Doonside Cup (L.), Ayr.
3rd Geoffrey Freer Stakes (Gr.2), Newbury.
Highland Spring Derby Trail Stakes (Gr.3), Lingfield Park.
Royal Whip Stakes (Gr.3), Curragh.
Henry II Stakes (Gr.3), Sandown Park.
Sire in UK and Japan.

Galant Vert

Won Prix de Lutèce (Gr.3), Longchamp.
Prix de Suresnes (L.), Longchamp.
Prix Juigne (L.).
San Marino Handicap (L.), San Marino.
2nd Hollywood Invitational Handicap (Gr.1).
Prix du Conseil de Paris (Gr.2), Longchamp.
Sire at Haras de Meautry.

Black Minstrel

Won seven races worth £32,080 including Earl of Chester Handicap.
Stallion in Ireland.

Djebel's son *Djeddah*, like Arbar, was bred in France by Marcel Boussac. A chesnut foaled in 1945 out of a mare named Djezima by Asterus, he won six races in France, and as a four-year-old won the Eclipse Stakes and the Champion Stakes in England. He was exported to America where his daughter Lalun won the Kentucky Oaks. He fathered several useful mares, including the dams of Proud Clarion (Kentucky Derby) and Never Bend, the sire of Mill Reef. His son *Midsummer Night II* won the Cambridgeshire Handicap at Newmarket.

Midsummer Night II, out of Nightsound by Mahmoud, was foaled in 1957, went to stud in 1963 and died in 1981. As well as winning the

Cambridgeshire he finished second in the Washington Singer Stakes at Newbury and in the Crocker Bulteel Cup Handicap (L.) at Hurst Park, and was third in the Dewhurst. He sired the winners of 189 races. His progeny earned £266,544 under National Hunt Rules and included Acquaint, Le Djinn, Midnight Fury, Summer Dance and Alverton who won the Cheltenham Gold Cup in 1979. Two other notable sons of Midsummer Night II are *Jimmy Reppin* and *Sula Bula*.

Jimmy Reppin foaled in 1965, had more success on the racecourse than his sire. He won the Sussex Stakes (Gr.1) and the Wills Mile (Gr.2), both at Goodwood; the Queen Elizabeth Stakes (Gr.2) at Ascot; the Hungerford Stakes (Gr.2) at Newbury (twice); the Prix Perth (Gr.2) at Saint-Cloud; the Coronation Stakes (Gr.3) at Sandown Park and the Queen Anne Stakes (Gr.3) at Royal Ascot. He also finished third in the 2,000 Guineas. He was exported to Sweden where he became a champion sire.

Sula Bula was foaled in 1978 when his sire was twenty-one years old. He was out of Blue Ann by Roadhouse. A 16.2hh bay horse, he was successful both on the flat and under National Hunt rules. His total winnings amounted to nearly £60,000. His successes included the New Year's Day Hurdle at Windsor and the Dipper Novices' Chase, and he was runner-up in the Haydock Park Champion Hurdle Trial and third in the Hurst Park Novices' Chase. He was retired to the Conkwell Grange Stud near Bath in 1986.

Other winners sired by Midsummer Night II include *Midsummer Star, Duky, Kruger* and *Quy. Midsummer Star* won the 2,000 Guineas Trial Stakes (Gr.3) at Ascot, was second in the Irish 2,000 Guineas at the Curragh, the Horris Hill Stakes (Gr.2) at Newbury, the Diomed Stakes (Gr.3) at Epsom, the Challenge Stakes (Gr.3) at Newmarket, the Hungerford Stakes (Gr.3) at Newbury and the Duke of York Stakes at York. He retired to stud in South Africa. *Duky* was a winner in Belgium, and *Kruger* in Italy. *Quy* won the Harewood Handicap (L.) at York and the Arrey of Leeds Spring Cup Handicap, before going to stud in Spain.

Galcador was yet another son of Djebel bred by Marcel Boussac. Foaled in 1947 out of Pharyva by Pharos, he was a medium-sized chesnut of good appearance and with a head resembling his Eastern ancestor. Out of his two starts as a two-year-old he won the Prix St Firmin at Longchamp. The following year he won the one-mile Prix Daphnis at Le Tremblay and then came second to Tantième in the French 2,000 Guineas. He then ran in the Derby, where he started at 100–9. He won by a head from Prince Simon. Those in the know expected a more convincing win and blamed his jockey, W. Johnstone, for challenging too soon. Galcador's racing days were over. He proved most disappointing at stud and ended his career in Japan.

Entente Cordiale, foaled in 1951, was owned by the 18th Earl of Derby. He was a bay colt out of Herringbone by King Salmon, grandson of The Tetrarch. Trained by George Colling, a master of his trade who had infinite patience, the colt won twelve races. His greatest triumph was the Doncaster Cup with champion jockey Doug Smith in the saddle. This unassuming and workmanlike jockey also piloted *Our Babu* to victory in the 2,000 Guineas in the same year – 1955. In fact he rode the winner of the Doncaster Cup no fewer than seven times. Entente Cordiale was retired to stud in 1956.

There can have been very few folk in the late 1940s who had not heard of *My Babu*. Whether it was his name (formerly Lerins), the glamour which his owner the Maharajah of Baroda conjured up, or his exploits on the Turf, is a matter for conjecture. Maybe the sight of an animal who was definitely non-utility lightened the days of austerity, but well known he was. Foaled in France at the end of the war out of Perfume II by Badruddin, he was bred by Peter Beatty at the Haras de Lion in Normandy. His breeder sold a half share to Prince Aly Khan. Then in 1946, when My Babu was a yearling, the Maharajah of Baroda saw him

Sula Bula winning the New Year's Day Hurdle Race at Windsor, January 1983.

whilst on a visit to France and was so struck by his graceful movement and air of quality that he bought him for 10,000 guineas.

He was sent to Fred Armstrong's stable at Newmarket. Previously based at Middleham, Armstrong moved to Warren Place which had been purchased by the Maharajah, so that constant journeys to Yorkshire would not interfere with his Highness's social life. My Babu was trained by the method of exercising horses little and often, and he responded well. He headed the Free Handicap with 9st 7lb. Included in his victories were the Woodcote Stakes at Epsom and the Champagne Stakes at Doncaster. In the New Stakes at Royal Ascot he dead-heated with Delirium, who went on to win the Prix Morny at Deauville.

OPPOSITE
The Maharajah of Baroda's My Babu ridden by Charlie Smirke, with his trainer before the 1948 Craven Stakes.

At the start of his three-year-old season My Babu won the one-mile Craven Stakes at Newmarket ridden by Charlie Smirke. During the 2,000 Guineas, which he won at 2–1 by a head from Cobbler, he strained himself severely. This, plus an anti-tetanus injection, caused stiffness and some swelling which interrupted his preparation for the Derby. He started favourite but it became evident that the distance was too great for him. He finished fourth behind My Love. He won the Sussex Stakes at Goodwood over a mile, but lost three weeks later to Estoc in a mile-and-a-half race at Goodwood. He was therefore withdrawn from the St Leger, as the distance was obviously beyond his capabilities. Reverting to a mile as a four-year-old, he won the T.F. Victoria Cup at Hurst Park in grand style, then the Craven Plate at Epsom. At the end of the season he retired to stud. He had won ten races and dead-heated in another and had earned prize money of £29,830. Notable winners of his in Britain included *Be Careful* (Gimcrack Stakes, Champagne Stakes), *Our Betters* (a winner in Britain and in America), *Primera* and *Our Babu*.

Primera, a strong, handsome bay, was bred at the Baroda Stud out of Pirette in 1954. He was bought as a yearling for 1,050 guineas by Mr C.H. Dracoulis, and trained by H. Wallington, for whom he won the Bridgewater Stakes in Salisbury and came second in the Irish St Leger. The following year, having been moved to Sir Noel Murless's stables, he won three races, including the important Churchill Stakes at Ascot over a mile and a half. He came second by a neck in the Princess of Wales's Stakes at Newmarket.

At five he became the property of Mr S.H. Joel, whose colours he carried to victory in the Ormonde Stakes at Chester, the Princess of Wales's Stakes and the Bentinck Stakes at Goodwood. He rounded off the season by winning the Ebor Handicap at York where he carried 9st. Altogether he won nine races worth £21,704. He came second in three races: the Churchill Stakes at Ascot, the Prix de l'Arc de Triomphe, half a length behind the winner, and in his second attempt at the Ormonde

Stakes. At stud he was more successful in siring fillies than colts. The most important of his fillies were: *Lupe* (Devonshire Stakes, Cheshire Oaks, Yorkshire Oaks, Coronation Cup, Princess of Wales's Stakes); *Aunt Edith* (Nassau Stakes, Prix Vermeille, Longchamp, Yorkshire Cup, King George VI and Queen Elizabeth Stakes); *Satu* (winner of £10,000 in France); *Prime Abroad* (winner of over £15,000 in France, and dam of Super Concorde); *Principal Boy* (winner of £13,000) and *Greengage* (winner of £18,000, including Coronation Stakes at Ascot).

Our Babu, foaled in 1952, was a bay colt out of Glen Line. Bred by Sir Oliver Lambart in Ireland, he somewhat resembled his ancestor Tourbillon, whose bent hocks were transmitted to many of his offspring. David Robinson bought him for 2,700 guineas and sent him to Geoffrey Brooke's Clarehaven Stable at Newmarket. Brooke had worked for many years with his brother-in-law, Atty Persse, and not surprisingly was an expert in bringing along early maturing youngsters. Such a one was Our Babu. He preferred good going, and the weather that season was kind to him. He won the Spring Stakes at Newmarket, the Champagne Stakes at Doncaster and the Middle Park Stakes at Newmarket just ahead of *Hugh Lupus*. He failed to win the Richmond Stakes at Goodwood, where the ground was soft, but finished the season heading the Free Handicap with 9st 7lb.

The following year he failed to win the 2,000 Guineas Trial at Kempton Park, but profiting from the outing he stormed home in the 2,000 Guineas itself, a neck ahead of Tamerlane, with *Klairon* not far behind. Subsequently he was unplaced in the Derby and finished only third to Tamerlane in the St James's Palace Stakes. His four victories amounted to £22,080. To take up his duties at stud, Our Babu crossed the Atlantic, having been purchased by a syndicate of American breeders. He sired over 170 winners worth $500,000. In 1963 he returned to England and was exported to Japan.

My Babu's son *Ginger Fizz* out of Effervescence was a chesnut colt foaled in 1962. He had a successful racing career for four seasons then went to stud. He sired many winners, including Lee's Chippy, Ginger Gale and Gin Fizz in Ireland. *Green Hornet, Pack Trip, Fusilier Boy, Garwol* and *Bronze Babu* were all horses by My Babu who succeeded on the racetrack in America. My Babu continued to sire winners until his death in 1970.

PART NINE

The English and Irish Heritage

The English and Irish Branch 1952 to 1984

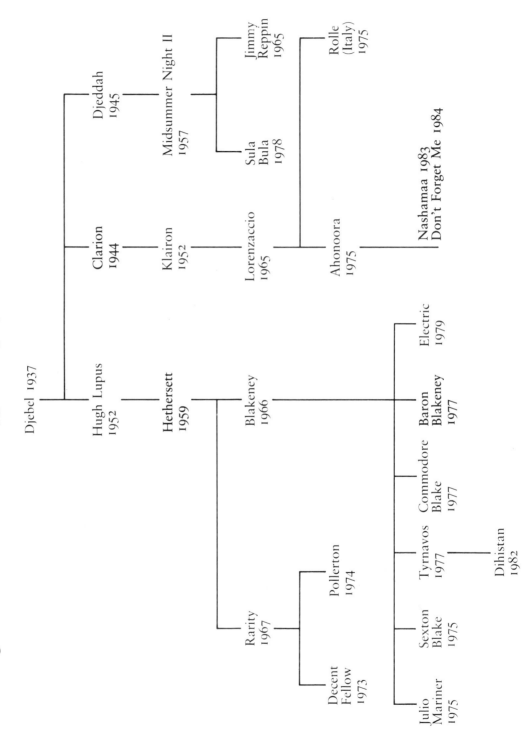

Djebel 1937

Hugh Lupus 1952

Djeddah 1945

Clarion 1944

Hethersett 1959

Klairon 1952

Midsummer Night II 1957

Blakeney 1966

Lorenzaccio 1965

Jimmy Reppin 1965

Sula Bula 1978

Rarity 1967

Decent Fellow 1973

Pollerton 1974

Ahonoora 1975

Rolle (Italy) 1975

Nashamaa 1983
Don't Forget Me 1984

Julio Mariner 1975

Sexton Blake 1975

Tyrnavos 1977

Commodore Blake 1977

Baron Blakeney 1977

Electric 1979

Dihistan 1982

1 | Hugh Lupus

DJEBEL'S SON *Hugh Lupus* and his grandson *Klairon* brought hope of the dynasty's continuance back to England once more. *Hugh Lupus*, though bred by the 2nd Duke of Westminster in France, spent most of his life on the English side of the channel. Foaled in 1952, he was a bay by Djebel out of Sakountala by Goya II. He was inbred in the second and third generation to Tourbillon, and in the third and fourth to Brûleur. Trained in Ireland by J. Lenehan, he was a top class two-year-old, winning the Testimonial Stakes and the Railway Stakes at the Curragh. In England he missed winning the Middle Park Stakes by a whisker, conceding victory to Our Babu, another of the Turk's descendants.

As a three-year-old Hugh Lupus won the Irish 2,000 Guineas by four lengths and was second in the Irish Derby and the Madrid Plate at the Curragh. So it was decided to run him in the English 2,000 Guineas. Accordingly he set off by 'plane, but somewhere over the Irish Sea Hugh Lupus became so restive that the pilot had no alternative but to turn back to Dublin. After this, it was planned to run him in the Epsom Derby, but a bruised heel put paid to that idea. At four, trained by Sir Noel Murless, he won five of his eight races. He excelled over any distance up to a mile and a half and won £15,233. At stud he had a low fertility rate, the fact that he was so in-bred probably accounting for this deficiency. Of the foals which he did sire, two were Classic winners, Pourparler, who won the 1,000 Guineas, and *Hethersett*.

Hethersett was bred and owned by Major Lionel Holliday, a Yorkshire manufacturer of decided opinions and an unrivalled knowledge of bloodstock breeding. He was rarely satisfied with his trainers and jockeys, who came and went with monotonous regularity. Nevertheless he was judged to be the great English owner-breeder of the post-war years. His bay colt out of Bride Elect by Big Game, a speedy filly as a two-year-old, was foaled in 1959 and grew to be both handsome and powerful. He was named Hethersett after a village in Norfolk. As a two-year-old he won the Duke of Edinburgh Stakes at Ascot very convincingly. This was his first appearance on a racecourse and augured well for the future. At three he had no difficulty in beating the opposition in the Brighton Derby Trial, which must have pleased his owner, crusty though he was. At 9–2 he started favourite to win the Epsom Classic. Ridden by Harry Carr, a competent and conscientious jockey, all went well until the descent to Tattenham Corner. But then Romulus fell bringing down other runners, including Hethersett, and the race went to Larkspur. Fortunately Hethersett was not seriously damaged, and he returned home to continue his training. Harry Carr was not so lucky; he sustained a broken shoulder and was unable to ride for a spell.

Hethersett went on to win the Great Voltigeur Stakes from Miralgo, but many folk doubted his ability to stay the distance in the final Classic, the St Leger. His connections had no such qualms. Ridden again by Harry Carr, one of the few jockeys of whom Major Holliday approved, he romped home four lengths ahead of his nearest rival, relegating Larkspur, the Derby winner, to sixth place. As a four-year-old he switched trainers from Major Dick Hern to S. Meaney. He ran three times but was unsuccessful on each occasion. His brief career at stud ended in 1966, at an early age of seven. Had he lived he would have made a great contribution to the dynasty. As it was he left behind *Blakeney*, *Rarity*, *Highest Hopes*, whose best performance was in the mile and a half Prix Vermeille at Longchamp, worth over £47,000, and another son *Hibernian*. This colt won the Beresford Stakes and the Irish Cambridgeshire, both run at the

Hugh Lupus in 1961.

Curragh. He was then shipped to America where he won over £23,000.

Rarity, out of Who Can Tell by Worden II, was foaled in 1967. He was an attractive bay with black points standing 15.3hh. He developed into a determined racehorse. In Ireland, he won the Athboy Stakes and the Desmond Stakes in which he beat Practicante by six lengths. At Four he defeated Lombardo by four lengths in the Group 3 Desmond Stakes and won the Ballymoss Stakes, also Group 3. In October he crossed the Irish Sea to compete in the mile and a quarter Champion Stakes (Group 1) at Newmarket, against formidable opposition. That day it rained in torrents rendering the ground sticky and soft. The chief danger was Brigadier Gerard, a horse of great quality and courage but with a dislike of soft ground. The last furlong was a battle royal. Brigadier Gerard's determination and the skill of his jockey, Joe Mercer, won the day but Rarity finished only inches behind.

He retired to the Ballygoran Stud in County Kildare, where he was held in high esteem by all. He sired very good-looking stock, including One in a Million, winner of the 1979 Ladbroke's Nell Gwynn Stakes and the 1,000 Guineas. Her daughter Milligram by Mill Reef won the Queen Elizabeth II Stakes at Ascot in September 1987 in impressive style, storming past the considerable opposition of Miesque, the hitherto invincible filly

Hethersett and W.H. Carr.

from France, and Sonic Lady. Rarity was the sire of ninety-six individual winners, whose successes included Group races. He was particularly noted for getting excellent brood mares, and was responsible for the dams of Hallgate and Nomination, as well as Milligram.

Personality-wise he was a great character, gentle and easy to manage. Patrick Headon tells of a 2.00 am visit to his box at the request of two French vets, where he demonstrated these qualities by lying full length on the stallion's back, his head on the horse's rump. Gentleman that he was, Rarity did not turn a hair though no doubt he curled his lip, as he was wont to do at the slightest provocation.

When it came to cattle it was quite another matter. One fine morning saw him turned out in his paddock. Someone had forgotten to move the bullocks, for which he had an intense dislike, from the next field. Seeing one grazing beside the railings he leaned over and grasped it firmly by the scruff of its neck. Up and down the railing he charged until the unfortunate beast was well nigh exhausted. The love of his life was an old grey mare, who helped on at least one occasion in the covering of a valuable broodmare. Rarity was very often in no hurry to consummate the union, and on one occasion showed no interest whatsoever. Not until the old grey mare was paraded before him (and whisked away at the last moment) would Rarity consent to cover his aristocrat visitor.

His stud career ended in 1984, when pain in his hind fetlocks led to his being put down. This unsung hero of the Turf was laid to rest under the green turf of Ireland, where he had earned so much respect and affection.

Winners sired by Rarity include:

Decent Fellow
Won John Porter Stakes (Gr.2), Newbury.
    Larkspur Stakes (Gr.3), Leopardstown.
2nd Ormonde Stakes (Gr.3), Chester.
4th John Porter Stakes (Gr.2), Newbury.
Also successful over hurdles.
Featured Stallion 1987, standing in Ireland.

Icelandic
Won Beresford Stakes (Gr.2), the Curragh.
    John Porter Stakes (Gr.2), Newbury.
    Gladness Stakes (Gr.3), the Curragh.
    Chester Vase (Gr.3), Chester.
    Rank Cup Handicap (L.), Phoenix Park.
Sire in New Zealand.

Camiros

Won Belgian Derby (Gr.1), Boitsfort.
Grande Poule des Produits (Gr.1), Groenendael.
Belgian St Leger (Gr.1), Groenendael.
Poule d'Essai des Poulains (Gr.2), Sterrebeek.
Prix Grisard de la Rochette (L.), Groenendael.

Pollerton

Won Princess of Wales' Stakes (Gr.2), Newmarket.
Gordon Stakes (Gr.3), Goodwood.
Scandinavian Open Championship (L.), Klamepenborg.
Sire of flat and National Hunt progeny.
19th in list of leading National Hunt sires of 1986.

2 | Blakeney

OPPOSITE
Blakeney winning the
1969 Derby.

BLAKENEY BY HETHERSETT out of Windmill Girl by Horn-beam, was foaled in 1966. According to his owner-breeder, Arthur Budgett, the wire which brought news of his birth stated that he was 'a small and rather ordinary first foal'. However, he developed into a particularly good-looking and proportioned bay colt, standing 15.2½hh. He was sent as a yearling to the Newmarket Sales where he failed to reach the moderate reserve of 5,000 guineas. Budgett's stud groom, Deakin, who was very fond of the colt, was bitterly disappointed at his rejection. He stated at the time that he knew he had the best yearling in the sale yet hardly anyone bothered to look at him.

So, Arthur Budgett decided to take him into training himself. He was 'a good doer and an easy horse to train'. They found some difficulty in choosing a name for him until someone suggested Blakeney, a village in Norfolk. His sire Hethersett had also been named after a Norfolk village and his dam Windmill Girl suggested a beautiful windmill reputed to be at Blakeney. Actually, the nearest windmill is at Cley-next-the-Sea, a few miles away, but Blakeney he is and the village must be proud of him.

He ran twice as a two-year-old, finishing fourth behind Caliban in the six-furlong Clarence House Stakes at Ascot in September, and a month later winning the seven-furlong Houghton Stakes at Newmarket in a field of twenty-seven. His jockey that day, Ernie Johnson, was promised the ride in the Derby, should the colt run. All did not go well in the spring of his third year. Blakeney was not himself and preparations were held up. He did, however, run in the Lingfield Derby Trial (Gr.3) on 16 May when, in spite of a storming finish he failed to beat The Elk. Nevertheless, it was decided that he should take his chance in the Derby.

The television crew, headed by Julian Wilson, visited the yard to film Blakeney for the Derby preview. Impeccably behaved as a rule, the colt was led out to pose for a shot outside his box. Head lad Tom Dowdeswell, who regularly rode him out, was given a leg-up. As he touched the saddle Blakeney gave an enormous buck for the first and only time in his life, unceremoniously dropping his partner. His owner declares that he 'just did it for the fun of the thing'. What Tom thought is not recorded!

Come Derby Day Blakeney as usual was keenly interested in everything around him. It took Ernie Johnson quite some time to get him down to the start because he kept stopping to observe all the sights on Epsom Downs. But once there he knew what was expected of him. He started the race at 15–2. At Tattenham Corner he was tenth behind Moon Mountain. Johnson, on the rails, made a bold bid for home two and a half furlongs out. Shoemaker and Moon Mountain were fighting it out ahead. The former veered slightly towards the stands and through the opening came Blakeney responding gamely to pressure. He gained the lead well inside the final furlong and beat Shoemaker by a length. Great was the triumph of one of the smallest colts to win the Derby and his delighted connections. Deakin, his confidence fully vindicated, watched with tears in his eyes as his favourite was led into the winner's enclosure. Then Blakeney, who like his dam always insisted on being backed up the ramp into the horsebox, was driven home to Whatcombe to a hero's welcome.

Unfortunately this triumph did not last. He did very little during the rest of the season. At the beginning of his four-year-old campaign he came fifth in the Jockey Club Stakes at Newmarket and then won a moderate Ormonde Stakes (Gr.3) at Chester. He ran a brave race in the Ascot Gold Cup, finishing second to Precipice Wood by three-quarters of a length. Racing again over a mile and a half in the King George VI and Queen Elizabeth Stakes (Gr.1) he made a bold bid but found Nijinsky too much for him and was beaten two lengths. In the Prix de l'Arc de Triomphe (Gr.1) he finished fifth behind Sassafras and Nijinsky.

Blakeney then retired to stand at the National Stud outside Newmarket having earned £66,641. He was rated 'the best of his age in Europe at a mile and a half' in 1970. At first he was a shy breeder but, like most of his progeny, he improved with age. By 1987 his offspring had won 670 races worth £2,900,000. In 1989, at the age of twenty-three, he was still covering his quota of mares and still taking a keen interest in the goings-on around him. On rainy days he could be seen peering out from the nearest shelter, refusing to budge until he was sure that the last drop had fallen!

One of the first of Blakeney's foals to win a Classic race was Juliette Marny. She won the 1975 Oaks at Epsom at 12–1 and the Irish Guinness Oaks at 5–2. She was also first past the post in the Oaks Trial Stakes (Gr.3) at Lingfield and third in the Yorkshire Oaks (Gr.1).

Following her came her full brother *Julio Mariner*, foaled in 1975 out of Set Free by Worden II. Owned by Captain Marcus Lemos, he probably owed his name to the Captain's seafaring interests. A handsome bay colt, he went into training with Clive Brittain. There he was fortunate to enjoy sympathetic treatment from both his trainer and the head lad M.J. Leaman. The latter, who had been with Brittain since their days as apprentices with Noel Murless, established an instant rapport with all his

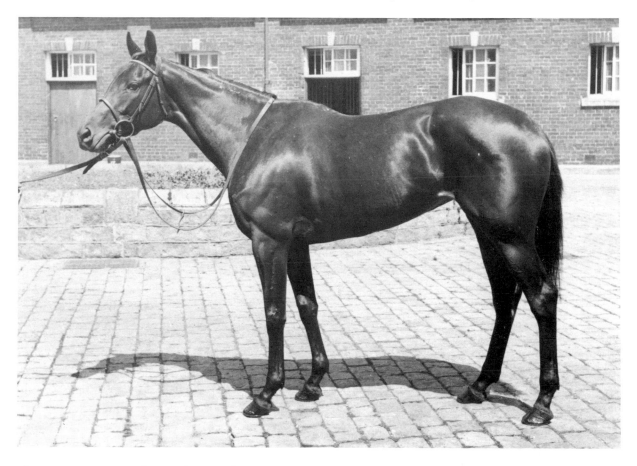

charges. Returning home from riding out, he would slip from the saddle and Julio Mariner would follow him round like a dog wherever he went.

The colt raced well on any ground and loved to 'lay into a bend'. His enthusiasm, however, made it essential to hold him up in a race. The right formula was finally applied when he won the St Leger at 28 1. Who knows what further successes he might have achieved had he not been sent to stand at Ashley Heath Stud, Newmarket, at the end of his third season in 1979. He had won three races worth £75,000.

Tyrnavos, out of Stilvi by Derring Do, was foaled in 1977, the result of a mating that was only decided upon after long discussion. Blakeney's dam Windmill Girl had been highly strung, and Stilvi, one of the best race mares of her generation and destined to become one of the greatest brood mares of modern times, was temperamental. However, it was finally decided to mate Blakeney with Stilvi and hope for a happy outcome. The bay foal which they produced grew into a colt of undoubted ability, with a front resembling his sire and a rear the image of his dam. He was a

Julio Mariner and E.
Hide.

lovely individual, friendly, honest and docile, though he could not bear
to be restrained and tended to react violently if he became upset. Thanks
to the understanding treatment of Bruce Hobbs and his stable, he won
£164,764 at two and three years old, over distances from seven furlongs
to a mile and a half. His successes included the Irish Sweeps Derby at the
Curragh, the Ladbroke Craven Stakes (Gr.3) at Newmarket, second place
in the William Hill Dewhurst Stakes (Gr.1) at Newmarket and fourth in
the Mecca-Dante Stakes (Gr.2) at York.

He retired to the Gazeley Stud in 1981 and was exported to Japan three
years later, leaving behind him winners of forty-six races worth £181,688,
including Dihistan, War Day and Tatra (Fr.) *Dihistan*, out of Damosa by
Abdos, was foaled in 1982 and was a twelve-length winner of the Clive
Graham Stakes at Goodwood, won the Hardwicke Stakes (Gr.2) at Royal

The Tetrarch in 1914, by A.G. Haigh.

Le Levanstell at Trimblestown Stud in Ireland.

Blakeney at the National Stud, Newmarket, in 1966.

Petrullo, photographed as a foal. He was sired by Electric and carries on the Byerley Turk line.

Ascot, the September Stakes (Gr.3) and the Gran Premio del Jockey Club (Gr.1) in Milan, as well as finishing third in the Royal Whip Stakes at the Curragh.

Electric, a bay colt out of a mare named Christiana by Double Jump, was foaled at the Moreton Paddox Stud. He was raised in the Warwickshire countryside until mid-summer 1980, when the process of moving stables to Stowell Hill, Templecombe, Somerset necessitated his early removal to Newmarket to be prepared with the other yearlings for Tattersall's Sales. It was hoped that his temperament, unlike so many of Christiana's foals, would prove tractable. Fortunately, this was so and he developed into a colt of 'marvellous quality and an absolutely excellent temperament' of which Robert McCreery, his breeder, was justly proud. He was a big, strong colt standing 16hh when fully grown and found no difficulty in attracting attention at the sales. He was sold to Michael Stoute to be trained for Raymond Clifford-Turner. So confident was Mr McCreery in Electric's ability that he expressed the wish to have a share in him if the new owner was agreeable. This resulted in his acquiring a quarter share. Electric won the White Rose Stakes (Gr.3) at Ascot, followed by the Gordon Stakes (Gr.3) at Goodwood. He was successful in the Great Voltigeur Stakes (Gr.2) at York, beating Diamond Shoal and Touching Wood (USA). He won the Jockey Club Stakes (Gr.3)

Electric at Whitsbury Manor Stud in Hampshire.

at Newmarket, finished second in the Coronation Cup (Gr.1) at Epsom, where Be My Native (USA) proved just too good for him, and in the Highland Spring Derby Trial Stakes (Gr.3) at Lingfield Park was third to Jalmood (USA). Unfortunately from time to time Electric suffered a serious problem with his back which, on a number of occasions, prevented him from doing himself justice. He retired to the Whitsbury Manor Stud in Hampshire in 1984, with earnings to his credit of £111,567. There his calm and relaxed attitude made him a pleasure to deal with.

Some winning sons and daughters of Blakeney

Mountain Lodge
Won Jefferson Smurfitt Memorial, Irish St Leger (Gr.1), the Curragh.
     Tote Cesarewitch Handicap, Newmarket.
3rd Doncaster Cup (Gr.3).
4th Henry II Stakes (Gr.3), Sandown Park.

Band
Won Yorkshire Cup (Gr.2), York.
     Cumberland Lodge Stakes (Gr.3), Ascot.
2nd Jefferson Memorial Irish St Leger (Gr.1), the Curragh.
2nd Prix Royal Oak (Gr.1), Longchamp.
3rd Jockey Club Stakes (Gr.2), Newmarket.
Sire in India.

Commodore Blake
Won Premio Ribot (Gr.2), Rome.
     Prix Perth (Gr.3), Saint-Cloud.
2nd September Stakes (Gr.3), Kempton Park.
2nd Land of Burns Stakes, Ayr.
3rd Prince of Wales' Stakes (Gr.2), Royal Ascot.
3rd Prix du Prince d'Orange (Gr.3), Longchamp.
Sire in South Africa.

Hunston
Won Queen Charlotte Handicap (Gr.2), Meadowlands.
     Matchmaker Stakes (Gr.2), Atlantic City.
     Cheshire Oaks (Gr.3), Chester.
2nd Flower Bowl Handicap (Gr.1), Belmont Park.
3rd Knickerbocker Handicap (Gr.3), Aqueduct.
3rd Lupe Stakes, Goodwood.
4th Lancashire Oaks (Gr.3), Haydock Park.

Satco (Fr)
Won Prix Berteux (Gr.3), Chantilly.
4th Grand Prix de Paris (Gr.1), Longchamp.
4th Prix de Lutèce (Gr.3), Longchamp.

Radiance (Fr)
Won Prix Corrida (Gr.3), Saint-Cloud.
2nd Prix de Royallieu (Gr.3), Longchamp.
4th Prix de Royaumont (Gr.3), Chantilly.

Two of Diamonds
Won Dee Stakes (Gr.3), Chester.
2nd Joe McGrath Memorial Stakes (Gr.1), Leopardstown.
2nd Classic Trial Stakes (Gr.3), Sandown Park.
2nd Ormonde Stakes (Gr.3), Chester.
4th John Porter Stakes (Gr.2), Newbury.

Tintagel
Won Prix Corrida (Gr.3), Saint-Cloud.
  Prix Fille de l'Air (Gr.3), Saint-Cloud.
2nd Prix Chloe (Gr.3), Evry.
3rd Prix de l'Opéra (Gr.2), Longchamp.
3rd Prix de Flore (Gr.3), Saint-Cloud.

Al Kuwait
Sire in New Zealand.

Baron Blakeney
Won Great Metropolitan, Epsom.
  Syd Mercer Memorial Trophy, Warwick.
4th Doncaster Cup (Gr.3).
Won Daily Express Triumph Hurdle (Gr.1), Cheltenham.
  John Wainwright & Co Chase, Warwick.
  Selsey Novices' Chase, Selsey.
  Alex Stanley Babs Wareham Novices' Chase, Newton Abbot.
  Cystic Fibrosis Novices' Chase, Liverpool.
3rd Sean Graham Hurdle, Liverpool.
Retired to stud 1984.

Coloso
Won Grand Prix Memorial Duque de Toledo (Gr.1), Madrid.
  Premio Corpa (Gr.2), Madrid (three times).

2nd Copa de Oro de San Sebastian (Gr.1), San Sebastian.
Gran Premio Memorial Duque de Toledo (Gr.1), Madrid.
Copa de S.M. El Rey (Gr.1), Madrid.
Premio Villamejor (Gr.1), Madrid.

Norfolk Air

Won Ladbroke Derby Trial Stakes (Gr.3), Lingfield Park.
Doonside Cup (L.), Ayr.
2nd Great Voltigeur Stakes (Gr.2), York.
Sire in New Zealand.

Sexton Blake

Won Laurent Perrier Champagne Stakes (Gr.2), Doncaster.
Seaton Delavel Stakes, (Gr.3), Newcastle.
Gordon Stakes (Gr.3), Goodwood.
Westbury Stakes (Gr.3), Sandown Park.
2nd William Hill Dewhurst Stakes (Gr.1), Newmarket.
Joe McGrath Memorial Stakes (Gr.1), Leopardstown.
Great Voltigeur Stakes (Gr.2), York.
Sire in Ireland.

3 | Lorenzaccio

LORENZACCIO, BRED by Captain A. D. D. Rogers in Ireland, was a chesnut colt foaled in 1965 by Klairon out of Phoenissa. Phoenissa had won a few races at two and three in very moderate company, but her sire The Phoenix was beaten only once in his career, in the Irish St Leger. He was judged the best two-year-old of his year and went on to win the Irish 2,000 Guineas and the Irish Derby.

When fully grown Lorenzaccio stood 16.1hh. He was an 'imposing chesnut with great presence, attractive with an effervescent personality'. To see him at full gallop was to witness 'the nearest thing to flight'. He was as highly strung as his Italian artist namesake probably was and proved quite a handful on the racecourse and later at stud. In the colours of Charles A.B. St George, black, white chevron and cap, and trained by Henry Cecil, he was a promising two-year-old, winning the six-furlong July Stakes at Newmarket by two lengths and finishing second in the Prix Morny at Deauville and the seven-furlong Champagne Stakes at Doncaster in course record time. At three he won the Prix Jean Prat over nine furlongs, was second in the Free Handicap Sweepstakes at Newmarket and third in the Queen Elizabeth II Stakes at Ascot. As a four-year-old he came second three times, in the Royal Hunt Cup carrying top weight of 9st; in the William Hill Handicap Stakes at Sandown, and in La Coupe de Maisons-Laffitte (Gr.3) in France, where he was beaten by Karabas.

Staying in training for a fourth season, he was better than ever, winning five times from eight starts. He was successful in the ten-furlong Prix Prince Chevalier at Saint Cloud by four lengths; the Prix de la Fouilleuse over a mile at Saint Cloud by six lengths; the Prix Quincey also over a mile at Deauville; the eleven-furlong Prix Foy at Longchamp, where he beat Schönnbrun and Prince Regent in a course record time of 2 minutes 15.6 seconds. Finally, the crowning glory of his career came in the Champion Stakes (Gr.1) at Newmarket, where he defeated the great Nijinsky, covering the mile and a quarter in 2 minutes 5.3 seconds. He retired to stud in 1971 having won nearly £88,000.

The first brochure from the Aston Upthorpe Stud shows a portrait of his head only. He danced and jigged so much that the photographer

Crested Wave, a leading Australian stallion and descendant of Electric.

found it impossible to take a full length shot of him! He was not the most ardent of suitors and often demanded all the patience of his handlers to persuade him to cover his mares. Nevertheless, he was not short of partners, even enjoying Royal patronage. He was joint-leading sire of two-year-olds in England in 1975. His first three crops won seventy-five races worth £112,489. His progeny raced successfully in the United States, Australia and Italy. They included:

Brewery Boy
Won S. Australian Derby (Gr.1).
      Victoria Derby (Gr.1), Flemington.
3rd W. Australian Derby (Gr.1), Ascot.

Rolle
Won Premio Presidente della Repubblica (Gr.1), Rome.
Sire in Australia.

Don Remon
Won W. Australian Sires Produce Stakes (Gr.2), Ascot.
2nd Melvista Quality Stakes (L.), Ascot.
      W. Australian Golden Jubilee Stakes (L.), Ascot.

Don Lorenzo
Won Niagara Handicap (Gr.2), Fort Erie.
3rd Valedictory Handicap, Greenwood.

Lord Paddington
Won Canterbury Cup (Gr.3), Canterbury, Australia.

My Klaire Berry
Won Premio Lazio (Gr.3), Rome.
    Premio UNIRE (Gr.3), Naples.

Cowan
Won Premio Sette Colli (L.), Rome.

Habeebti
Won Hillsborough Handicap, Bay Meadows.
3rd Autumn Days' Handicap, Santa Anita.

Zaccio
Champion American Steeplechaser.

But Lorenzaccio's most famous son, sired before he was exported to Australia, where he died at the age of twenty-one, was Ahonoora.

Lorenzaccio winning the Champion Stakes at Newmarket in 1970.

4 | Ahonoora

AHONOORA! The Egyptian war-cry has sounded over the courses of England and beyond, challenging the might of the Darley Arabian dynasty. Foaled on 12 April 1975, out of a Martial mare named Helen Nichols, Ahonoora was bred by the Wyld Court Stud. David Richer remembers that 'as a foal he was rather weak and narrow, certainly not the robust, strong sort one would imagine a high-class sprinter to be.' As a yearling he started to fill out and caught the eye at Tattersall's October Sales. Always an exceptionally good walker, he fetched £7,600. He developed into a handsome, rangy, dark chestnut colt standing 16.1hh, and was a friendly, gentle individual both in and out of the stable.

As a juvenile he won once and was placed second twice from his three starts, winning a Maiden at Newbury in June second time out. Unfortunately, in July he split a pastern and was unable to race again that season. At three he ran nine times, winning twice. His characteristic explosive start and willingness to try his best were well displayed in his sensational victory in the Spillers Stewards' Cup, when he started at 50–1 and beat Double Form. As a four-year-old he won a handicap at Newbury, the King George Stakes (Gr.3) at Goodwood, the Windfields Sprint Handicap at Epsom and the William Hill Sprint Championship at York, all over five furlongs. He was defeated by three-quarters of a length in the King's Stand Stakes (Gr.1) at Royal Ascot and in the Vernon's Sprint Cup (Gr.2) at Haydock Park. On both occasions the winner was Double Form, the subsequent champion sprinter.

Jockey Frank Durr remembers him as a 'fantastic character who loved racing and had a big heart'. He always put his utmost into his work and hated to be beaten or whipped. Once at Ascot, while he was running his heart out, the jockey struck him. He resented this so much that on his return to the stable he sulked for a fortnight. No friendly head looked over the door, no whicker of welcome greeted his lad. He presented his backside to the world in silent protest.

He retired to the Irish National Stud in 1980 at the modest fee of IR £2,250, later rising to £2,750. His physique was 'ideal for breeding'. He possessed 'good bone, plenty of muscle, splendid quarters, neck and forearm'. But he was not expected to produce any progeny other than commerical two-year-olds and sprinters. To everyone's surprise, and to the delight of his managers, his first crop contained five stakes winners: *Ahohoney* (Prix Fille de l'Air [Gr.3], twice at 10½ furlongs, value £8,533; three-year-old winnings in France £18,245; four-year-old winnings, £13,256); *Princess Tracy* (Ballyogan Stakes [Gr.3], Baroda Stud Phoenix Spring [Gr.3]); *Leysh* (Cambridgeshire); *Camps Heath* (Ayr Gold Cup); *Babillard* (four races in Brazil, including the Grande Premio Duque de Caxias [Gr.2]).

In his second season, Ahonoora sired Noora Abu, Miss Noora and Ardassine, all promising, together with *Park Appeal*. This dark brown filly, sold for only 6,600 guineas as a foal, fetched 62,000 guineas as a yearling, largely due to her half-sister Desirable's success in the Cheveley Park Stakes (Gr.1) at Newmarket. She proved to be worth every penny. As a two-year-old she was unbeaten in four starts, including the Cheveley Park Stakes (Gr.1), the Moyglare Stud Stakes (Gr.1) at the Curragh and the Oldtown Stud Stakes at Phoenix Park. She finished the season as champion filly in England and Ireland. After an uneventful third year she departed to

Ahonoora and G. Starkey winning the Tote Credit Handicap in 1979.

North America, where she held her own in stakes' company, winning the Country Queen Stakes at Hollywood Park.

Ahonoora's third crop were three-year-olds in 1986. They included Ala Malik, Nashamaa and Park Express. *Ala Malik*, a chesnut filly out of Negligence by Roan Rocket, was unbeaten at two and only very narrowly beaten in Tattersall's Musidora Stakes (Gr.3) at York. She came home a length and a half behind the winner in the 1,000 Guineas. Continuing her career in the United States, she was soon amongst the first three in graded races. *Nashamaa* a brown colt out of Balidaress by Balidar, a full brother to Park Appeal, won once at two and as a three-year-old collected prize money of £335,535. He won the Breeders' Cup Classic Trial at Phoenix Park and came second in the BBA (Ireland), Goff's National Stakes (Gr.2) at the Curragh. He retired to the Ardoon Stud in 1988. The pick of the bunch was another brown filly named *Park Express*, who proved her sire capable of producing good middle distance runners as well as sprinters. A big rangy filly out of Matcher by Match III, Park Express was rated top two-year-old filly in Ireland. At three she collected £325,014 by winning four times and being placed five times. Her successes include The Phoenix Champion Stakes (Gr.1) at Phoenix Park, the Harp Lager Lancashire Oaks (Gr.3) at Haydock Park and the Vodafone Nassau Stakes (Gr.2) at Goodwood. It seemed as if Ahonoora's fame was to rest on the merits of his fillies until in 1986 a two-year-old colt appeared on the racing scene, named *Don't Forget Me*.

In six years Ahonoora sired the winners of eighty-four races at home worth £894,708 and eighteen races abroad worth £73,858. He stamped his stock very well and most of them, as was their sire, are of a placid disposition. He became leading sire in England and Ireland in 1986 and in 1987 commanded a stud fee of IR £20,000. He was syndicated in 1989, but had to be put down later in the year, following an accident in Australia.

5 | Don't Forget Me

Don't Forget Me, the colt with the evocative name, was bred by Mrs Frances R. Hutch in Ireland. Foaled in 1984, he is the second foal of African Dolly by African Sky, a Sing Sing horse. His name was chosen for him in a much more mundane way than imagination leads us to suppose. At the time travellers to the farms in Ireland were not held in very high esteem, and on departing minus an order would remark, 'Well, don't forget me!'

The colt developed into a striking bay of about 16hh and was known in the stables as 'The Big Horse'. He was bought for a mere 19,000 guineas at the Tattersall's Open October Yearling Sales and went into training with Richard Hannon. Willie Carson tells of the time when he first rode the colt on Mr Cunningham Brown's gallop, six furlongs slightly up-hill. He thought he had a moderate handicapper under his saddle until it was time to pull up – then Don't Forget Me started to go. He realised that here was no 'flashy worker' but a genuine colt of considerable potential. Richard Hannon describes him as honest and a 'grand horse to deal with'. Normally a very relaxed horse, he goes to work with a will when it matters most.

He first carried Jim Horgan's colours of pink with a black sash and striped cap as a two-year-old. He won the last three of his four starts. He led most of the way in the Lanson Champagne Vintage Stakes at Goodwood and six weeks later fought off the challenge of Deputy Governor to win the Laurent Perrier Champagne Stakes (Gr.2) at Doncaster.

The following season he was in the Craven Stakes (Gr.3) at Newmarket. Tenacious though he was he could not catch Ajdal but it was hoped that he could turn the tables in the General Accident 2,000 Guineas sixteen days later.

Two 'planes had been chartered to take the Horgan family from Cork to Newmarket, and hopes were high for a successful meeting. But on the colt's arrival it was discovered that he had spread a plate in the worst possible way: it had twisted inwards and severely bruised the sole of his foot. Mike O'Gorman, the vet, made a dash across country and after examining the foot thought that the colt might have a fifty-fifty

Don't Forget Me and Willie Carson on their way into the winners' enclosure at Newmarket after winning the 2000 Guineas in 1987.

chance of running. An equine foot jacuzzi was loaned by Mick Ryan, the Rutland Arms donated all their ice and the patient animal stood in the swirl for five hours. Still it was by no means certain that Don't Forget Me would race. Luca Cumani's blacksmith made a special plate and the colt was led quietly round the parade ring on the grass. Willie Carson, who was to ride him, received very clear instructions: 'If he feels wrong when you get down to the start, withdraw him.'

However, he seemed to be sound and duly lined up with the others – a formidable array who included Ajdal, Bellotto, Most Welcome, Risk Me and Midyan. Brave, tough and determined, Don't Forget Me jumped off in front and like an arrow, flew down the centre of the course. He was challenged and challenged again, but Don't Forget Me hated to be passed. To the cheers of the crowd (many of whom had a lump in their throat) he stormed home in the excellent time of 1 minute 37 seconds. Racing folk admire courage and here was a colt who had proved his worth and lived up to his noble heritage. On 16 May he lined up again, this time for the Airlie Coolmore Irish 2,000 Guineas. He led throughout the race to become the first horse since Right Tack in 1969 to complete the Anglo/Irish Guineas Double.

His racing days over, Don't Forget Me, retired to the Coolmore Stud in Ireland, where his services are employed, thus ensuring the continuation of the Byerley Turk line.

PART TEN

Continuation

'AND GOD took a handful of South Wind and from it formed a horse saying "I create thee, O Arabian. To thy forelock I bind victory in battle, on they back I set a rich spoil, and a treasure in thy loins. I establish thee as one of the glories of the earth. I give thee flight without wings" ' (Translated from the Arabic)*.

This inheritance has endured down the ages. Sometimes obscure, often predominant, the characteristics of fire, intelligence and a tractable disposition, mingled with the intrinsic qualities of the tough and courageous native hobby or running horse – for it must not be forgotten that the contribution of the hardy Galloway mare is of equal importance – have designated British bloodstock as the most famous and sought after in the world. There can be no doubt that the influence of the intrepid Byerley Turk and his stalwart partners will continue as long as man's association with the racehorse abides.

In the words of a fifth-century poet of the Nejd Bedouins: 'Are not these an inheritance from our fathers? Shall we not to our sons in turn bequeath them?'

* *The Classic Arabian Horse*, by Judith Forbis.

Advertised Stallions for 1988, Great Britain and Ireland

by Blakeney: Rowlandson 1973, Baron Blakeney 1977, Layal 1979, Lucky Mickmooch 1973, Rushmere 1973, Electric 1979, Blakeney Point 1978, Sexton Blake, 1975.
by Luthier: Black Minstrel 1974, Over the River (Fr.) 1974, King Luthier 1982.
by Levmoss: Riot Helmet 1973, Telsmoss 1976.
by Lorenzaccio: Ahonoora 1975, Point North 1978, Brewery Boy 1978.
by Ahonoora: Nashamaa 1983, Don't Forget Me 1984, Dromod Hill 1983.
by Rarity: Decent Fellow 1973, Rare One 1973, Pollerton 1974, Venetian Gate 1975, King's Ride 1976, Long Pond 1981.
by Hethersett: Blakeney 1966, Heres 1967.
by Klairon: Antwerp City 1973.
by Le Levanstell: Netherkelly 1970, Garryowen 1975, Le Moss 1975.
by Midsummer Night II: Hey Romeo 1971, Duky 1974, Sula Bula 1978.

Index

Names in *italics* refer to horses. Page numbers in *italics* refer to illustrations.

Lincolnshire College of Agriculture and Horticulture
Library
Caythorpe